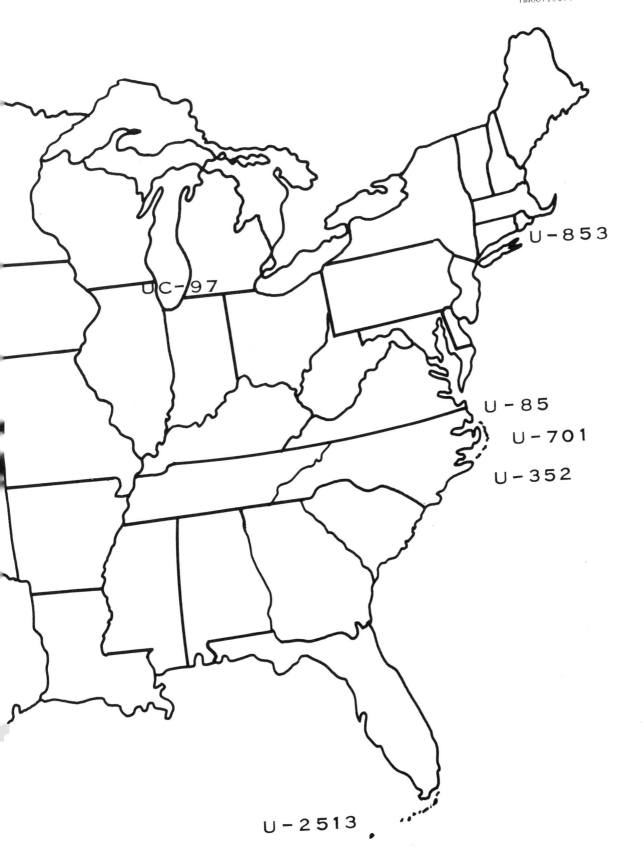

U-853

U-85

U-701

U-352

UC-97

U-2513

Dive Into History

U-boats

Dive Into History

U-boats

By Henry Keatts and George Farr

AMERICAN MERCHANT MARINE MUSEUM PRESS
United States Merchant Marine Academy
Kings Point, New York

International Standard Book Number 0-936849-03-7

Published by
American Merchant Marine Museum Press
United States Merchant Marine Academy
Kings Point, New York

Distributed by

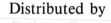

AQUA QUEST PUBLICATIONS, INC.
Post Office Drawer A
Locust Valley, NY 11560-0495
(516) 759-0476

Cover photograph of U-352 *courtesy of and copyright by Jon Hulburt*

Printed in Hong Kong

To the men of the United States
Merchant Marine who served despite the
menace of Germany's U-boats
during both World Wars.

PUBLISHER'S NOTE

Dive Into History — U-boats is the first of a multi-volume work, "Dive Into History." The series will comprise a history of shipwrecks selected for their accessibility to amateur U. S. scuba divers. That constraint excludes many interesting vessels more than 250 feet underwater. *Dive Into History — Warships,* the second volume of this series is being prepared for publication. Requests for information should be addressed to Professor Henry Keatts, Suffolk County Community College, Riverhead, New York 11901.

PREFACE

More than a century has elapsed since Jules Verne captivated would-be underwater explorers with his fanciful concept of the submarine in *Twenty Thousand Leagues Under the Sea*. It is unfortunate that the engineers, designers, and marine architects who ultimately developed his dream into workable submarines were more guided by political, economic, and warfare concerns than was the hospitable Captain Nemo. His *Nautilus* was designed primarily for peaceable exploitation of the sea. Her progeny proved the terrible effectiveness and tactical advantage of undersea vessels almost immediately after the outset of World War I. Imperial Germany's U-boats provided that demonstration, and they did so through the use of vessels that were relatively primitive compared to the capabilities of the fictional *Nautilus*.

Only two months into the war, Germany's *U-9* torpedoed and sank three of Britain's armored cruisers, *Aboukir, Cressey,* and *Hogue*. Disbelief swept the world at the news; a submarine of only 493 tons, manned by a crew of 25, had swept more than 36,000 tons of heavily armed warships with 1,460 men into oblivion in less than one hour. Most remarkable was that it was accomplished by a U-boat that was already deemed obsolete by the Germans. A new dimension had been added to naval warfare — scrapping all existing naval strategies.

The U-boat developed into the basic offensive weapon of the German Navy in both World Wars. One of the most decisive military conflicts in the history of mankind, termed by Winston Churchill, the "Battle of the Atlantic," pitted Germany's World War II submarine fleet against the combined military and merchant sea power of the Allies, primarily Great Britain and the United States. That confrontation extended far beyond the waters of Europe before it ended. Prior to World War I, a trans-Atlantic crossing by a submarine would have been considered the wildest fiction. But before that war ended, U-boats were attacking Allied shipping along the United States coast with great success. During World War II,

such crossings were commonplace, thanks to dramatic advances in Germany's submarine development.

The repeated successes of marauding U-boats drove the United States into the development of strategic and technological counter-measures that accounted for the sinking of many U-boats that had penetrated American waters. Those historic wrecks have joined their victims in stimulating a "cottage industry" along the east coast. Enterprising boat captains have discovered a ready market for chartering their boats to groups of amateur scuba divers who are anxious to explore the sunken U-boats and other ship-wrecks off the Atlantic shore of the United States.

Grand Admiral Karl Dönitz fondly referred to his country's U-boats as wolves of the ocean. Wolves they were indeed while they prowled the seas, but resting on the bottom, ravaged by time and deterioration, they are only harmless skeletons of wolves. Still, their shadowy outlines in the gloom of ocean depths manage to strike fear; many divers will admit to a skipped heartbeat in the menacing presence of a sunken grey wolf.

Shipwrecks emit a siren song to sport divers, those amateur historians, photographers, salvagers, and souvenir hunters who eagerly travel hundreds of miles at great expense for a brief visit. But distance matters little measured against the opportunity to spend moments with sunken relics — to dive into history.

This volume has not been written as an academic treatise, but one imperative that has been rigidly observed is historical accuracy. If incorrect data, mis-interpretation, undue emphasis, or lack of information exist, we would welcome correction by our readers who recognize those failings. It would be fruitless, even damaging, to perpetuate a misleading historical record. Additional information, forwarded to Professor Henry Keatts, Suffolk County Community College, Riverhead, New York, 11901, will receive appreciative attention and confirming research for inclusion in further editions of this work.

ACKNOWLEDGMENTS

The authors gratefully acknowledge the contributions and cooperation of the following individuals and organizations:

H. A. Yadnais, Jr., Dr. Dean Allard, and their staffs, Naval Historical Center.

Frau Lenk, WZ-Bilddienst, Wilhelmshaven, West Germany.

R.M. Coppock, Naval Historical Branch, Ministry of Defence, London, England.

National Archives.

Submarine Force Library and Museum, Groton, Connecticut.

The Mariner's Museum, Newport News, Virginia.

Harry J. Kane III, Harris Publications, Inc., for approval to include two illustrations from "Eagle" magazine.

Fred Benson, Tom Roach, Ed Caram, Mike Casalino, Steve Bielenda, and Michael A. deCamp for use of their outstanding photographs. We are especially grateful to Tom Roach who granted several long interviews and permitted review of correspondence from Kapitänleutnant and Frau Sommer.

Executive Dean R. David Cox and Professors Dan Murray and Lucas Carpenter, Suffolk County Community College, for editorial assistance.

Jeff Miller and Bill Kurz for film printing services.

Scuba divers George Purifoy and Larry Keen for sharing their experiences.

Aaron Hirsch for his many helpful suggestions on the book's layout.

Colette Napoli and Doreen Leed for typing assistance.

TABLE OF CONTENTS

PART I

HISTORICAL SETTING

CHAPTER ONE

U-BOAT EVOLUTION

By the mid 1890's, Germany under Kaiser Wilhelm II had prospered to become the second greatest trading nation in the world, yet her navy ranked only fifth. Wilhelm held no illusions about his country's place in international commerce. He was fully aware that such domination is fleeting. More than two thousand years earlier, the Phoenicians surrendered their 700 year trade leadership when the Greeks surpassed them as a maritime power. Germany's trade was not to suffer the same fate for the lack of a strong navy. Wilhelm would see to that.

The Kaiser called upon the genius of his country's leading industrialist, Friedrich Alfred Krupp to provide the needed sea strength. Krupp responded with the acquisition of Germania Werft, an established shipyard in Kiel. That new facility added to Krupp's factories in Essen, Annen, Rheinhausen, and Magdeburg equipped him to furnish vessels from rivets to armament. He did just that, contributing a formidable addition of nine battleships, five light cruisers, and thirty-three destroyers to the Imperial Navy in the period leading up to World War I. During that time, Germany's foreign trade prospered, with imports more than doubled and a three-fold increase in exports between 1890 and 1913.

During the build-up of Germany's naval might, Grand Admiral Alfred von Tirpitz would have nothing to do with the unproven and, in his estimation, unneeded submarine. He looked upon such underwater weaponry as essentially defensive — and Germany's irregular coastline lent itself to more conventional defenses. Krupp's engineers did not share those views and, over von Tirpitz' objections, they conducted experiments with underwater boats. The Grand Admiral was not alone in his assessment. For years, the United States and France had spearheaded the development of submarines solely for harbor defense purposes. They persisted, while the German Navy dragged its heels in adopting the submarine. But once Germany did accept it, she was to lead the world in exploiting the offensive potential of the deadly underwater weapon.

GERMAN SUBMARINE DEVELOPMENT

The glamour of underwater travel had stimulated the inventive genius of creative Germans for centuries before World War I. A diving boat had even been designed by a Nuremberg weapons engineer named Kyeser as far back as 1465. That early beginning led to seventeenth and eighteenth century developments that included a technical description of a diving boat in 1604 by a teacher from Rostock and an unsuccessful diving boat that was commissioned by Karl von Hessen in 1691. In 1772, a 40-foot oar (surface) and fish tail (submerged) propelled boat was commissioned by Count Wilhelm of Schaumburg-Lippe as an addition to his fleet on Lake Steinhuder along the northern border of his principality.

By 1792, J.A. Schultes, Professor of Medicine at Landshut, had considered the problem of providing fresh air underwater; he proposed a chamber of air bottles to resolve the problem. Six years later, a German named Klingert constructed an adjustable depth diving platform to accommodate a man wearing a water-tight suit and diving helmet. Then, in 1799, a mine surveyor, Joseph von Baeder, published his plans for a two-man submarine. But Germany would not see an underwater vessel that could be considered a submarine, free of umbilical cords and capable of extended underwater travel, until the ninteenth century.

Wilhelm Bauer. Courtesy of Submarine Force Library and Museum.

Sebastian Wilhelm Valentin Bauer, a 27-year-old non-commissioned artillery officer in the Bavarian Army, had been developing plans of a submarine when he left for the Army of Schleswig-Holstein in January 1850. His new commanders were apparently more impressed than the Bavarians. They authorized him to build a small model powered by a clockwork mechanism. When that was completed, it incorporated all the essentials of later submarines and led to the authorization for a full-sized boat, the 26.5-foot *Brandtaucher* (Sea Diver). The constraints of a limited budget persuaded Bauer to modify the submarine's specifications against his better judgement. The critical hull thickness and frames strength were each reduced by half. As a result, the hull collapsed at a depth of thirty feet instead of its originally designed 100 feet.

The crippled submarine lay inert on the bottom trapping its three-man crew inside for five long hours. Escape through the hatch was blocked by the outside water pressure that resisted every effort to push it open. Only Bauer's ingenuity, saved his own and his two crewmen's lives. When the oxygen was almost depleted, he opened the sea cock and water rushed in until the trapped air was compressed to equal the outside pressure. Then the hatch opened easily, so easily, that it flew open in a massive burp of released air that carried the three to the surface in a bubble, the world's first recorded escape from a sunken submarine.

That occurred on February 1, 1851. Her crew had been saved but *Brandtaucher* was to remain on the bottom for another thirty-six years while the significance of her advanced design impressed itself on the nation. Then, in 1887, the "old lady" was raised and painstakingly restored to be put on display at the Berlin Naval Museum in 1906. After follow-on displays at Rostock and Potsdam, while two major wars were being contested, she was again restored between 1963 and 1965 before she was moved to Dresden where she has been proudly exhibited since 1973.

The Danish war, for which *Brandtaucher* had been built, ended with the 1850 Treaty of Berlin. Bauer's efforts to convince the German government to finance another submarine fell on unresponsive ears. However, another war was on the horizon. The Crimean War between Russia and England threatened, offering him a new opportunity. Bauer left for England in 1853, there, to be welcomed by Queen Victoria's prince consort, Prince Albert, and his team of engineering advisors: Lord Palmerston, John Scott Russell, Isambard K. Brunel, and Charles Fox.

Bauer was assigned to work with the British engineering team to design and construct a submarine for the British Navy. He willingly threw himself into the task with no qualms of allegience. After all, his own government had already turned him down and the impending war did not involve Germany. But another, more personal, concern soon intruded. It was clear that his colleagues were exploiting him, and that he would not tolerate. He fled England, leaving behind some of his ideas, but depriving the British of his guidance. The project continued without him, but the only distinction the resulting vessel earned was a place in naval records as the first true submarine to lose its entire crew.

With the outbreak of the Crimean War, Bauer's allegience gave him even less of a problem. He owed the British nothing at all. He left for Russia, where he obtained financing for the construction of an improved version of *Brandtaucher*. The submarine, *Le Diable Marin* (Sea Devil), Bauer's third, including the London venture, was launched at St. Petersburg on November 1, 1855. The 52-foot boat was driven by a screw propeller powered by four men walking a treadmill. It was

Bauer built the 26½ foot *Brandtaucher* (Sea Diver) in 1850. Courtesy of Submarine Force Library and Museum.

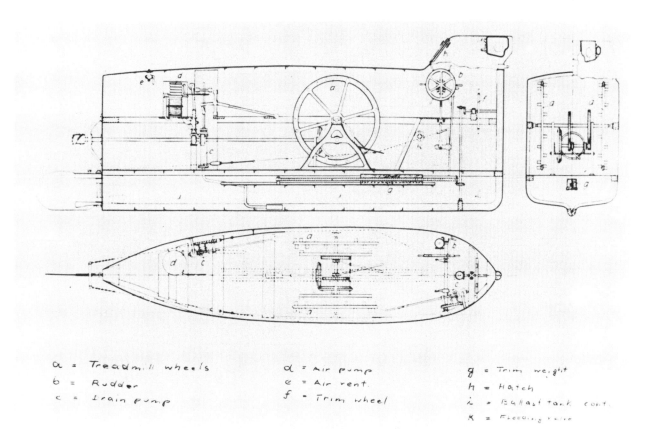

a = Treadmill wheels
b = Rudder
c = Train pump

d = Air pump
e = Air rent
f = Trim wheel

g = Trim weight
h = Hatch
i = Ballast tank cont.
k = Flooding valve

Inside *Brandtaucher*'s conning tower. Courtesy of Submarine Force Library and Museum.

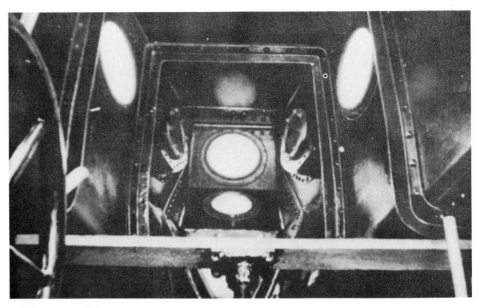

Brandtaucher was propelled by turning two large wheels which were located amidships. Courtesy of Submarine Force Library and Museum.

Bauer's *Brandtaucher* had a sliding weight for submergence and depth control. Courtesy of Submarine Force Library and Museum.

armed with a 500 pound explosive charge, not unique in itself, but the means of deploying it was. A crewman inside the vessel put his arms into a pair of shoulder-length rubber gloves attached to the bow in order to transfer the timed explosive charge to the hull of the target ship.

The quality of Bauer's design is attested to by the fact that he and his crew of thirteen made 134 trial dives, one to a reported depth of 150 feet. An inept Russian lieutenant was responsible for the boat swamping on her last dive. She was raised, but the Russians never bothered to restore the submarine to working order. Undeterred, Bauer introduced radical changes into a larger submarine that he hoped would gain the support of Russia's naval leaders. It was to be propelled by steam on the surface and compressed air when submerged. Armament included 24 cannon, but not even that heavy fire power swayed the uncompromising opposition of the Russian Navy. Bauer didn't realize how serious his opposition was until he learned of plans to move him and his project to Siberia. He left for Munich without delay. His ambitious project was never completed.

Wilhelm Bauer in Russian uniform with his wife. Courtesy of Submarine Force Library and Museum.

Le Diable Marin (Sea Devil), Bauer's third submarine, was built for the Russian Navy. Like *Brandtaucher,* she was driven by a screw propeller but the new submarine was powered by four men walking a treadmill. Courtesy of Submarine Force Library and Museum.

Bauer's final contribution to submarine development was *Kustenbrander* (Coastal Incendiary), a 412-ton underwater fighting ship equipped with armor-piercing armament of his own design. The vessel incorporated an internal combustion engine, the first step to the turbine system requiring no outside air that one day would follow — a tribute to Bauer's advanced thinking.

Between 1867 and 1870, a small, 17-foot underwater boat was built by another German, Frederich Otto Vogel, at the Schlick Yard in Dresden. Its significance lies in the use of a steam engine specially adapted for submerged propulsion. How well it may have performed remained unanswered when the vessel sank during her first trials in the River Elbe. Two other submarines, one in 1885 and the other in 1890, are reported to have employed steam-electric propulsion. Information on these boats and their performance is sparse; it is known that each was about 115 feet long but not how well they operated.

A German torpedo-engineer, Karl Leps, is credited as having designed an experimental submarine that was probably never subjected to diving trials because it had no air renewal or ventilation system and the hull was not watertight, the latter a likely reason for many electrical failures. The boat was built by the Howalt Yard at Kiel in 1897 and is referred to as either "Howalt Diving Boat, Construction Number 333" or more simply "Leps diving boat." It rates mention primarily because it was propelled by a non-reversible 120-hp electric motor powered by a bank of batteries built into the bottom of the hull.

TWENTIETH CENTURY

A Spanish engineer, Raymond Lorenzo d'Equevilley-Montjustin, submitted his plans for an experimental submarine to the French Naval Ministry in 1901. When they were rejected, he offered them to Germany through the Krupp firm, then busily engaged in building the strength of the Kaiser's Navy. His design was almost identical to that of Maxime Laubeuf, a brilliant French engineer with whom d'Equevilley had been associated in Paris. Laubeuf had transformed the submarine from a defensive device to a long range weapon of offense with the introduction of his advanced design double-hull underwater boat in 1899. Krupp was impressed by what d'Equevilley offered and was apparently not concerned with its similarity to Laubeuf's concept. A long term contract was signed to have d'Equevilley start preliminary work in February, 1902.

Admiral von Tirpitz refused to budge. He rejected Krupp's request for funds to pursue the submarine project.

Determined to continue, Krupp financed the work at his company's expense. The keel of the 15.5-ton boat was laid on February 19, 1903; the submarine was completed less than four months later, on June 8. But somewhere in the process, much of the similarity to Laubeuf's advanced design was lost, including the use of a double-hull.

Yard trials between June 23 and December 6 proved that the new, single-hull, 43-foot boat handled well after some initial problems were corrected. Her operating radius was 25 nautical miles at four knots, and she could operate underwater at 5.5 knots. A 65-hp electric motor provided both surfaced and submerged propulsion. However, the boat was powered by batteries that had to be removed for recharging. For that reason, she always had to be berthed close to a mother-ship or a shore power station. That may account for the fact the submarine was equipped with lifting padeyes (metal rings welded to the deck) so she could be raised aboard larger warships. Observation was provided by a platform forward of midships equipped with a small, adjustable Zeiss periscope. Diving and compensating tanks were fitted to the boat, and underwater control was achieved by hydroplanes fore and rudder planes attached to a stabilizing plate aft. Two compressed air tubes for firing 18-inch torpedoes were fitted at the sides. One problem that remained unresolved was that seawater rushing into the evacuated tube after a torpedo firing caused the craft to list as much as 20 degrees.

The Kaiser demonstrated his personal interest in the new vessel by observing it conduct a submerged attack against a target moored three miles away. Two months later, on September 23, a proud crew greeted Prince Henry of Prussia as he boarded for a brief cruise. The Prince is even credited with having handled the controls of the experimental boat.

Admiral von Tirpitz remained unimpressed.

Early in 1904, war between Russia and Japan influenced Russia to purchase the Krupp boat that had been turned down by the German Navy. She was christened *Forelle* for commissioning into the Russian Imperial Navy. Russia's newest submarine was first transferred to Petersburg (Leningrad) and then, by train, to Vladivostock. There are no Western records of her participation in the Russo-Japanese War, or even of her ultimate disposition.

Russia's agreement with Krupp included not only *Forelle* but also three more boats, an order that would bear a heavy influence on German submarine development. Like earlier submarine builders, Krupp engineers recognized the shortcomings of each new boat while it was still being assembled. Work had already been started on the design of a larger submarine, one that would eliminate *Forelle's* problems of battery powered electric motor propulsion. The internal combustion engine was combined with the electric motor and engine fuel was stored outside the working compartments. Fuel explosions and fire had plagued the gasoline powered boats of other navies. That exposure would now be minimized by isolating fuel storage which would also dramatically lessen the risk of incapacitating the crew with leaking fumes.

A double-hull design with fuel stowed outside the pressure hull had been patented by d'Equivilley in 1904. It was adopted for the new boats. Krupp's countryman, Rudolph Diesel, had patented a new design for a heavy-oil engine that might also have been incorporated into the program. However, Krupp selected another German firm, Körting Brothers, to develop kerosene engines for the submarines. Körting's reputation had been built on the production of small, 8-hp kerosene engines for use in automobiles and launches. The decision in favor of kerosene was to hinder German submarine development for the next eight years. The delay might have been even longer had not Krupp engineers conducted their own diesel experiments during the short era of kerosene-fueled submarines.

Körting eventually produced six sets of 200-hp kerosene engines, two for each of the three Karp class boats ordered by Russia as part of the *Forelle* deal. The three submarines, *Karp, Karas,* and *Kambala,* each displaced 207 tons and could make 10.8 knots. The kerosene engines produced enough power, but fuel consumption was high and engine durability was low. A further disadvantage lay in the large exhaust funnel that dominated the outline of the boat. It had to be raised before operation and lowered for stowage before diving. Despite those shortcomings, Krupp's new boats ushered in a bright new era of submarine safety with their use of kerosene and exterior fuel tanks.

BIRTH OF THE U-BOAT

Krupp's demonstration of the new design accomplished the near-impossible. Admiral von Tirpitz was finally convinced that it was time for the German Navy to have a submarine of its own. Till that time, Russia had financed Krupp's efforts, but von Tirpitz' support provided a German Navy appropriation of 1.5 million Marks ($292,000) for submarine development.

The German Navy's first submarine was unimaginatively christened *Unterseeboot-eins* (underwater boat #1). *U-1* was launched August 4, 1906 with Oberleutnant Bartenbach in command of a nineteen man crew. She was a somewhat improved and slightly enlarged (234 tons) version of the three Karp class boats, but she proved to be an indifferent success. The speed of the 139-foot boat was 10.8 knots surfaced and 8.7 knots submerged. She was armed with an 18-inch bow

Admiral von Tirpitz, alongside Kaiser Wilhelm (right), was initially opposed to the German Navy funding submarine construction. Courtesy of WZ-Bilddienst, Wilhelmshaven, West Germany.

9

torpedo tube and carried three torpedoes. The real disappointment was her cruising range, specified as 1,500 miles but limited by endurance tests to so much less that it was considered dangerous to take her out into the open sea.

The second experimental U-boat, *U-2*, was built by the Imperial Dockyard at Danzig. The Navy Office required that she be larger, more powerfully armed, and higher powered than her predecessor. *U-2* was launched in June, 1908, ten feet longer and 100 tons heavier than *U-1*. Although she was equipped with more powerful engines (600-hp) and 630-hp electric motors, her endurance was no greater than *U-1*'s. Four torpedo tubes, two bow and two stern, did provide the new model with a decided armament advantage over the one tube *U-1*.

Two other boats, *U-3* and *U-4*, were built in Danzig during 1908, a reflection of the new emphasis being placed on submarines by the government. They were almost 100 tons heavier than *U-2* (420 tons) and carried a 37mm deck gun. But even before the two were launched, the Navy Office established a rigid set of specifications for those that were to follow:

  . Surface radius of 2,000 miles at high speed
  . Two bow and two stern torpedo tubes
  . Capacity for at least six torpedoes
  . Speed of 15 knots surfaced and 10.5 knots submerged

The German Navy ordered fourteen more boats, *U-5* through *U-18*, between 1908 and 1910. Speed proved to be the most elusive requirement.

The Korting kerosene engines still could not produce more than 300-hp, and they continued to be unreliable. Even in sets of four, the engines were inadequate for the 188-foot boats with their 500 tons displacement and crew of four officers and twenty-four men. *U-9*, for example, could produce 14 knots surfaced but no more than 8 knots submerged. Only the last three, *U-16*, *U-17*, and *U-18*, attained the specified 15 knots surface speed, but engine breakdowns occurred in proportion to the higher speed. All shared the kerosene drawback — the tremendous tower of smoke that belched from their stacks while the engines were in operation. But even with those limitations, *U-9* was to demonstrate the power of Germany's new offensive undersea capability early in the First World War.

The potential of the Korting kerosene engine seemed to be exhausted and propulsion improvement was essential if U-boat development was to progress. Krupp's foresighted Germania Werft engineers provided the solution from the Diesel engine experiments they had begun in 1906. The Maschienenfabrik-Ausburg-Nurnberg (M.A.N.) Company was also developing a Diesel engine that was even better than Krupp's. Perhaps the diesel program was still considered to be exploratory when the first diesel-engined submarine was built in Germany. That might explain why it was produced, not for the Fatherland, but for Italy. The *Atropo*, completed by Krupp in 1912 for the Italian Navy, was powered by two small, experimental 350-hp diesel engines. By contrast,

The German Navy's first submarine was unimaginatively christened *Unterseeboot-eins* (underwater boat #1). The dense column of white smoke from the kerosene burning U-boat could be spotted several miles away. Courtesy of Submarine Force Library and Museum.

U-19 was the first diesel powered U-boat for the German Navy, and the first truly seagoing U-boat. The fuel-efficient diesels gave her a range of 5,000 miles — four times that of *U-18*. Courtesy of WZ-Bilddienst, Wilhelmshaven, West Germany.

Germany's first diesel U-boats would have 850-hp engines. With that much power, U-boats of 650 tons could be considered feasible. No longer hampered by power limitations, *U-19* through *U-22* were fitted with two M.A.N. 850-hp diesels beginning in July, 1913. *U-19* had a range of 5,000 miles, four times that of *U-18*.

The next four U-boats, *U-23* to *U-26,* each 670 tons, were powered with two 900-hp Krupp diesels. The first, *U-23,* completed in September 1913, measured 210.5 feet and was armed with 19.7 inch torpedoes. Deck armament was increased to two 86mm guns. Evolution continued along already established lines — progressively longer, greater displacement, more powerful diesel engines, increased operating range, and more formidable armament. By 1913 Germany's big ocean-going U-boats were a reality, only a decade after Krupp launched his first experimental submarine. Although the German Navy was still convinced that the value of the submarine would be primarily for defense, the entire world would soon learn the offensive might of the new undersea weapon — the single factor that almost won two major wars for Germany.

CHAPTER TWO

WORLD WAR I

Archduke Francis Ferdinand, heir apparent of Austria-Hungary, and his wife Sophie were victims of a Serbian nationalist assassin in the Bosnian town of Serajevo on the morning of June 28, 1914. That crime set off a series of events that would convulse Europe in four years of conflict that was to devastate a continent at a cost of 8 million military lives and more than 21 million wounded — the "Great War".

Europe had gradually polarized into two major camps over a period of 35 years — Germany with Austria-Hungary in one and France with Russia in the other. A web of other intangling alliances had also developed to set the stage for a major European confrontation. Assured of support from Germany, Austria-Hungary declared war on Serbia a month after the Serajevo murders. The assassination provided convenient justification for Austria to annex Serbia as it had Bosnia years before. Russia, committed to stand by Serbia, mobilized on July 30. Germany reacted by declaring war on Russia the following day. In a dizzying sequence of events, both Germany and France mobilized and Germany responded to French mobilization with a declaration of war against France on August 3. Europe's military leaders had for so long accepted the dictum "Mobilization means war!" that a confrontation was inescapable once the mobilization button was pressed.

Germany invaded Luxembourg and demanded free passage for her troops through Belgium. Belgium refused to compromise her sovereignty and said no. Britain, pledged to guarantee Belgian neutrality since 1831, mobilized immediately and declared war at midnight, August 4, even though Germany had not yet invaded Belgium. Both sides expected that the war would be quickly decided by land battles. Only when their armies were deadlocked did nations turn to the sea and their navies to break the stalemate.

Submarines were included in the navies of each major country when war erupted in August, 1914. France led with 123, but her diesel technology was inferior. Britain ranked second with 72, of which 17 were new, diesel-powered boats. Russia, with 41 inferior submarines, was third. The United States, fourth, had 34 submarines, 12 of them diesel. Germany's 26 U-boats ranked her fifth, but 12 of the 26 were diesel-powered and she enjoyed a rapidly advancing technology that would be highly responsive to military needs.

U-BOATS

Naval history was made in September 1914 by Korvettenkapitän Otto Hersing, commanding Germany's *U-21*, when he sank the first warship to be sunk by a self-propelled torpedo from a submarine. He sent the aptly named 2,940-ton British light cruiser *Pathfinder* and her crew of 259 to the bottom on September 5. She was to be the first of many.

It was Kapitänleutnant Otto Weddigen, however, who convinced even the most stubborn capital ship proponents of the lethal attack capabilities of the submarine. On September 22, with the war not yet two months old, Weddigen in command of *U-9*, an out-dated, kerosene-powered boat, sent three British armored cruisers — *Aboukir, Hogue,* and *Cressy* — to the bottom of the North Sea. The enemy cruisers were steaming a straight course at 10 knots without destroyer

Archduke Franz Ferdinand (left) and Emperor Franz Josef. The assassination of Ferdinand and his wife Sophie gave Austria-Hungary the excuse to declare war on Serbia, and "The Great War" began. Courtesy of National Archives.

escorts. A single torpedo was fired, striking *Aboukir* on the starboard beam. A column of water shot into the air and lookouts on the bridges of her two sister ships assumed that *Aboukir* had struck a mine. Following Royal Navy tradition, the cruisers braved the suspected mines and moved in to offer assistance.

The U-boat crew rearmed the empty tube. Ten minutes later, with all four tubes loaded, *U-9* maneuvered into position and fired her two bow torpedoes at *Hogue*. Discharging both at the same time lightened the boat so much that her bow broke the surface. Both torpedoes struck, but the U-boat was now discovered and *Hogue*'s guns immediately opened fire.

U-9 regained control, dove out of sight, and loaded her last reserve torpedo. Weddigen ordered her two stern tubes to bear on the third cruiser, *Cressy*. Lookouts, now alerted, spotted their foaming tracks as both torpedoes were fired. The cruiser maneuvered out of the path of one torpedo, but the second struck.

Artist rendition of the initial action between Germany's *U-9* and three British armored cruisers. HMS *Aboukir* is struck in the starboard beam by a torpedo. Courtesy of WZ-Bilddienst, Wilhelmshaven, West Germany.

Artist rendition of HMS *Cressy* being hit by a torpedo as HMS *Hogue* sinks in the background. Courtesy of WZ-Bilddienst, Wilhelmshaven, West Germany.

The triumphant return of *U-9* after sinking three British cruisers. Disbelief had swept the world at the news; a submarine of only 493 tons had sunk more than 36,000 tons of heavily armed warships with 1,460 men in less than one hour. Courtesy of WZ-Bilddienst, Wilhelmshaven, West Germany.

Weddigen observed the stricken warship from the submerged *U-9* while *Cressy*'s guns opened fire on the only exposed part of the U-boat, her periscope. Weddigen maneuvered through the fire and sent his last torpedo away for the coup de grace. It hit, and *Cressy* sank.

The entire action had taken less than one hour. Yet, in under 60 minutes, *U-9* had sunk three armored cruisers for a total of over 36,000 tons with a loss of 1,460 men. Germany hailed Weddigen as a national hero for his achievement; the Kaiser presented him with the Iron Cross 1st class; he and every member of the *U-9* crew received the Iron Cross 2nd class.

In the spring of 1915, Weddigen was lost in another U-boat, *U-29,* when she was rammed by the British battleship, *Dreadnaught.* Germany's naval hero joined his victims *Aboukir, Hogue,* and *Cressy* on the floor of the North Sea. Posthumously, Weddigen was awarded the Pour le Merite (Blue Max). That famous order, founded by Frederick the Great, was Germany's highest war decoration, and Weddigen was the first naval officer of the war to receive that honor. After his widely heralded success, submarines were recognized as more than merely defensive weapons. *U-9* had opened a new era in naval offensive warfare with one dramatic, three-pronged stroke.

The stunned British realized that unless captial ships were accompanied by an adequate anti-submarine escort of destroyers they would be seriously exposed to U-boat attack. But not until late 1915 were sufficient escorts available to screen the British battle fleet with any degree of effectiveness.

The Germans had produced a weapon to strike the enemy with a freedom denied to their surface

Kapitänleutnant Otto Weddigen wears the Iron Crosses he was awarded for sinking *Aboukir, Hogue,* and *Cressy.* He joined his victims on the floor of the North Sea when he was lost in *U-29.* Courtesy of WZ-Bilddienst, Wilhelmshaven, West Germany.

16

Kapitänleutnant Otto Weddigen flanked by the crew of *U-9*. Courtesy of WZ-Bilddienst, Wilhelmshaven, West Germany.

ships. A few U-boats had forced the most powerful navy in the world, the British Grand Fleet, to retreat from its unprotected anchorage at Scapa Flow. More important, the British had fled from the main theater of naval action — the North Sea.

COUNTER MEASURES

Early in the war, the only anti-submarine defenses available to the Allies were conventional deck guns and ramming tactics. Once below periscope depth, the U-boat was free from such attack. Then only mine fields and steel nets, often garnished with mines, posed a threat. However, during the first three years of war, British mines tended to be defective and nets could only be used in narrow waters such as the Straits of Dover. The nets extended only 60 feet below the surface, and U-boats could dive to depths of more than 150 feet. When the buoys of a net were sighted, it was no problem to dive safely below the threat. In addition, each U-boat was equipped with a saw-edged blade installed on its bow to cut through the steel mesh.

After *U-9* sank *Aboukir*, *Hogue*, and *Cressy*, the British Admiralty instructed all ships to zigzag and use their higher speeds while cruising in hostile waters. In addition, steamers, schooners, and trawlers were armed for use as decoys. They were intended as bait to lure a U-boat to the surface, close enough for the decoy to destroy her with hidden guns. In 1917, as many as 180 of these so-called Q-boats were searching for U-boats. The Germans, however, were wary; during the war, only 13 were destroyed by the decoy ships. Others suffered severe damage from encounters with the Q-boats, but they survived — testimony

to the ability of double hull U-boats to withstand heavy punishment.

The British quickly installed a chain of radio direction finding (RDF) stations to pinpoint the location of transmitting U-boats. But it was one thing to locate a U-boat and quite another to destroy her — until depth charges came into their own. They were reported in use as early as July, 1915 by two disguised armed trawlers, Q-boats *Gunner* and *Quickly*. Cylinders, called "ash cans," containing 300 pounds of explosive were

The Imperial Navy's U-boat Medal, *U-Bootsabzeichen*, usually awarded after several World War I operational patrols.

rolled off the stern and detonated by a hydrostatic valve at a pre-set depth. Later, devices were developed to catapult depth charges from a ship.

Another important Allied development was the hydrophone, a crude underwater listening device installed on ships or at shore stations to detect submarines travelling submerged. The devices were primitive, but they marked the beginning of a new era in anti-submarine warfare. A U-boat could no longer dive to escape her pursuers with a screen of water to cloak her movements.

In July 1916, a small minelaying U-boat became the first submarine to be sunk by a depth charge. *UC-7* was first detected by a hydrophone aboard the motor boat *Salmon*. For two hours, the hydrophone operator monitored an intermittent buzzing. As the volume increased, he reasoned that the U-boat was approaching. With good judgment and considerable luck, a depth charge was dropped overboard at the very moment *UC-7* passed underneath. The violent explosion that

brought debris boiling to the surface was probably due to detonation of mines carried by the U-boat.

Although depth charges seemed to be effective anti-submarine devices, their production was only 140 per week one year after *UC-7* was destroyed. However, by late 1917, output had accelerated, and the depth charge played a vital role in turning the tide against Germany's underwater fleet.

Anti-submarine offensive skills were also developed by Allied aircraft, and air patrols developed into a constant source of worry to the Germans, although only six U-boats were sunk by planes during the war. Airplanes were to serve as a much more effective measure against the undersea menace during World War II.

In October 1914, an important event in submarine history occurred when Kapitänleutnant Feldkirchner in *U-17* sank the first merchant ship, the British steamer *Glitra*. That action, the first against a non-military vessel, led to the concept of

Imperial Germany utilized the Belgium port of Bruges as a submarine base after occupying that country. Kaiser Wilhelm II is shown at Bruges in May 1918 with U-boat commanders, reflecting his avid interest in the Imperial German Navy throughout his reign. Courtesy of National Archives.

a U-boat blockade of Great Britain to throttle her lines of commerce.

Germany experimented briefly in 1915 with unrestricted submarine warfare, sinking neutral ships that ventured within specified war zones. On May 7 of that year, the British passenger liner *Lusitania* was sunk off the Irish coast with the loss of 1,198 lives, 124 American. The first unrestricted campaign fell short of expectations. In the first three months, only 33 ships totaling 100,000 tons were sunk. Those results and the American protests that followed the *Lusitania* disaster, prompted Germany to discontinue her campaign of unrestricted naval warfare.

In February 1917, Germany's self-imposed U-boat restrictions were dropped because the German Admiralty felt that Germany's only hope of winning the war was to sever England's supply line. The British were dependent on merchant shipping not only for war supplies but also for food and other vital necessities.

UNITED STATES ENTRY

On the third day of Germany's renewed unrestricted campaign, President Wilson broke diplomatic relations between the United States and Germany. Two months later, on April 6, 1917, the United States declared war.

The unrestricted submarine warfare campaign did not precipitate the end of the war as Germany had hoped. Rather, it converted the United States from contemplative, if biased, neutral to an active belligerent, hostile to Germany. Thus, the U-boat proved to be the indirect cause of Germany's defeat by its action in directing America's full industrial might, manpower, and naval strength against the Kaiser.

With the active participation of the United States, the Allies were in a position to cope with the U-boat menace by using escorted convoys. The technique had been operating successfully on a small scale, but with too few escort vessels available for meaningful effect. America's warships made large convoys possible barely in time to prevent Allied capitulation because of a shortage of critical supplies.

April, when the United States entered the struggle, marked the record monthly loss, almost 900,000 tons of Allied shipping sunk. Within one month that saw the first large convoy, sinkings were cut almost in half to 549,987 tons, but even that improvement was still far from acceptable. That start marked a trend that was to continue month by month until the following fall when convoys and increased production of depth charges turned the tide against the U-boat. Those measures effectively neutralized Germany's under-water campaign and every U-boat victory from then on was hard won.

Germany built about 390 U-boats during the war. Of those, 178 were sunk with the loss of 5,366 officers and men, nearly 40% of total U-boat personnel. In the final two years, improved anti-submarine tactics and weapons increased German losses to seven U-boats a month. Her shipyards, however, had by then accelerated production and were turning out new, improved boats faster than the earlier ones were lost.

For their part, U-boats accounted for 5,708 Allied ships totaling an incredible 11,018,865 tons. In addition to merchant shipping, 28 Allied capital ships (battleships and cruisers) were sunk.

During the course of the war, Germany developed large U-boats capable of crossing the Atlantic to harass the increasing volumes of men, munitions, and food that was flowing from America to bolster the Allied war effort. For the first time since the War of 1812, more than a century earlier, a foreign power brought naval hostilities to the coast of America. Six U-boats destroyed 165,000 tons of shipping in waters along the eastern seaboard from Newfoundland to Cape Hatteras. That action accomplished little to end hostilities in Europe, but it did provide an omen of long-range potential of the German U-boat.

WAR ENDS

By autumn of 1918, it was evident that Germany had lost the war. When, on November 5, the Allies announced their readiness to discuss the terms of peace, Germany readily accepted. Four days later the German people rebelled, and the government was turned over to the Socialists. When a German republic was proclaimed, Kaiser Wilhelm fled across the border into Holland. An armistice agreement ended hostilities on all fronts at 11 A.M. on November 11.

The Treaty of Versailles was signed on June 28, 1919. It differed from earlier European Treaties such as those of Utrecht or Vienna, where victor and vanquished met in polite disputation. France's Georges Clemenceau was bitter; he fought with savage intensity for drastic military and economic sanctions against Germany. The Germans were excluded from many of the more stormy sessions, and when the treaty terms were presented, no oral discussion was allowed. Written protests and counter-proposals were permitted, but only a few concessions were granted. Marshal Ferdinand Foch, also of France, prophetically observed regarding the Versailles Treaty: "This is not Peace. It is an Armistice for twenty years."

World War I was a proving ground for the war

that would follow. Almost a quarter century later, U-boats would once more prowl the sea lanes to creat chaos in shipping circles. Although the anti-submarine techniques of the first war would be useful, Allied victory would once again be achieved only after staggering sea losses threatened early defeat.

The signing ceremony of the Treaty of Versailles on June 28, 1919. The Treaty's severe military and economic restrictions on Germany produced divisions of opinion that permitted Hitler to violate its provisions with impunity. Courtesy of National Archives.

CHAPTER THREE

WORLD WAR II

With the end of the war in 1918, Germany lost all her U-boats; those that were not scuttled were surrendered to the Allies. The Treaty of Versailles provided for almost total disarmament of the defeated enemy. It also prohibited Germany from building or otherwise acquiring submarines, but many of Germany's trained designers were kept busy on submarines in Finland, Spain, Holland, and Sweden. Adolph Hitler's repudiation of the military limitations of the Versailles Treaty was greeted by U-boat designers with improved versions of boats that had been built abroad for foreign navies. It was unfortunate for Germany that her Admirals did not place greater emphasis on preparations for submarine warfare. Germany entered World War II as she had the first World War, with too few U-boats.

In further defiance of the Versailles Treaty, Hitler had developed an army to fulfill the objectives of *Mein Kampf*. Those troops marched into the Rhineland early in 1936 and again on March 11, 1938, into Austria. Two days later, the Führer announced the union of the two countries. Only a few months later, during the summer of 1938, Nazi demands were made on Czechoslovakia to surrender the Sudetenland, and Hitler made it clear that he was willing to risk war for it.

What were the Allies, who had paid such a high price for their victory, doing during this impudent series of surrender treaty violations? Great Britain's Prime Minister Neville Chamberlain, for one, adopted a naive policy of appeasement that led to an accord signed by Hitler, Chamberlain, Italy's Mussolini, and Deladier of France on September 30, 1938 in Munich. It presumed to avert war by accepting Nazi acquisition of the Sudetenland. Chamberlain, on his return to England, declared: "I believe it is peace for our time." That time was indeed brief. Germany followed by invading the remainder of Czechoslovakia on March 13, 1939. Heartened by the indications that England and France would not interfere, Mussolini, claimed his share of the spoils, ordering Italian troops to invade Albania on April 7, 1939.

With Mussolini's action, England and France realized the error of appeasement. When Hitler mobilized Germany's troops along the Polish border, both countries announced that any attack on Poland would mean war. Despite that warning, German troops invaded Poland on the morning of September 1, 1939. Two days later, France and Britain declared war against Germany. World War II had been launched. Untold millions would die or be maimed, cities and historic treasures would be obliterated, and atrocities would lay bare the worst side of man's nature.

BATTLE OF THE ATLANTIC

Many had predicted a second World War. One eminent military authority, Field Marshal Foch of France, predicted not only that there would be a war but further, "The next war will begin where the last one ended." Naval experts on both sides of the Atlantic agreed that submarine warfare and anti-submarine tactics would be a continuation of World War I. That conflict had seen U-boats finally neutralized by the convoy system and depth charges. In the period between the wars, the British introduced two new threats to the U-boat, the aircraft carrier and ASDIC. The latter is an acronym for the Anglo-French Anti-submarine Defense Investigation Committee, developer of

Karl Dönitz, Commander-in-Chief of the U-boat Arm. He exhorted his U-boat commanders: "U-boats are the wolves of the ocean. Attack! Rend! Destroy! Sink!" Their successful missions contributed to his January 1943 promotion as successor to Grossadmiral Erich Raeder, Commander of the German Navy (Kriegsmarine). At the Nuremberg trials, Dönitz and the U-boat branch were cleared of the accusations of war crimes. However, Dönitz did serve a ten-year sentence for having, in peacetime, trained his men to fight and having them ready to do so when war was declared, in violation of the Treaty of Versailles. Courtesy of National Archives.

the sounding system that the United States referred to as SONAR. Strengthened by those improvements in her arsenal, Britain was inclined to make light of the U-boat threat. Relatively low shipping losses in the early months of the war contributed further to that complacency.

With the fall of France on June 22, 1940, the entire strategic balance changed. Germany had gained ports to base her U-boats in occupied France, with an ocean front of 2,500 miles. At the outset of the war, Germany had only 57 U-boats and two of those were for training. No great submarine fleet had been built in preparation, but German designers were experienced and in-

novative. They were also highly responsive to changing defensive or offensive strategic requirements, a vital factor in the highly successful U-boat building program.

Both sides had entered the conflict unprepared, Germany with too few U-boats and Britain with only 180 destroyers. Germany held the advantage, however; the U-boat's increased operational area made the number of available escort vessels inadequate for the task of protecting convoys.

By 1940, Admiral Karl Dönitz, Commander-in-Chief, U-boats, was so heartened by the increased output of U-boats that he declared, "I will show that the U-boat alone can win this war.

In March 1941 Prime Minister Winston Churchill proclaimed the "Battle of the Atlantic." His purpose, like featuring the "Battle of Britain" nine months earlier, was to concentrate all Allied resources upon the U-boat war. Courtesy of National Archives.

Nothing is impossible to us." He almost accomplished his goal by modifying the tactics of World War I when U-boat commanders fought as individuals. During World War II, their activities were coordinated by radioed orders from the U-boat High Command on shore. Reconnaissance planes and patrolling U-boats informed Dönitz of convoy positions, and the information was relayed to U-boats that attacked, whenever possible, in packs rather than alone.

Dönitz had developed what he referred to as the "rudeltaktik" or wolf-pack. Radio communication would place members of a pack in positions around a convoy. Then, in a simultaneous attack, the U-boats would smash through the defenses of a convoy. Another tactic was to use surfaced wolf-packs in night forays. Using their low silhouettes to advantage, they would penetrate the perimeter of a convoy undetected, inflict punishment, and escape.

Hitler's action in 1935 to abrogate the military constraints of the Versailles Treaty had created a problem of deciding which type of U-boat would be built. German engineers offered several to choose from. The two best designs were the Type VII of 626 tons and the long-range Type IX of 1,032 tons. Although he had shrugged off the "shackles of Versailles," he did not want to

During German submariners' "Happy Time" of 1942, convoy PQ-17 left Iceland for Russia with 35 Allied merchant ships, and 21 escort vessels. This photograph shows a torpedo exploding against the hull of one of the 22 merchant ships that were lost during the passage. Courtesy of National Archives.

Attacks such as this on convoy PQ-17 resulted in the loss of 153 men, 430 tanks, 210 aircraft, and almost 100,000 tons of other war material, termed by Churchill to be "one of the most melancholy naval episodes in the whole of the war." Courtesy of National Archives.

antagonize Great Britain to the point where that nation might try to interfere with his program of military expansion. In 1935, the two countries signed the Anglo-German Naval Agreement to limit the total tonnage of submarines each of them would be permitted to include in their navies. Dönitz, compelled to adhere to that agreement, had to decide between the larger, long-range Type IX and the older, and smaller, Type VII. Obviously, more of the smaller Type VII's could be produced within the given tonnage limitation.

The smaller Type VII was chosen for mass production in order to provide sufficient numbers of U-boats to carry out Dönitz's wolf-pack tactics. Dönitz was convinced that the best place to defeat the British was along the western approaches to that island empire, and the range of the Type VII, though limited, was adequate for the task. Both the range and performance were extended during the war with the evolutionary changes in the Types VIIB and VIIC. The work-horse Type VII series was destined to become the most renowned U-boat of World War II. It proved to be a formidable offensive weapon, even though it was only a modest refinement of its World War I predecessors. By the time the war ended, a total of 705 boats of the Type VII variety had entered service.

The Kriegsmarine U-boat Medal, U-Bootsabzeichen, usually awarded after several World War II operational patrols.

British complacency quickly folded in the face of new U-boat tactics and the use of French ports as U-boat bases. Sinkings of Allied shipping reached 515,000 tons in March 1941 and the following month it climbed to 589,000 tons. For the next eight months, losses averaged 360,000 tons. During 1942, 6,250,000 tons were lost by the Allies, more than 40% of all losses to U-boats for the entire war. Allied shipbuilding could hardly replace losses of such magnitude and Dönitz was close to fulfilling his 1940 claim that the U-boat alone could win the war.

Winston Churchill, Britain's Prime Minister, in *The Second World War,* likened Britian's plight to that of "the diver deep below the surface of the sea, dependent from minute to minute on his air pipe. What would he feel if he could see a growing shoal of sharks biting at it?"

TIDE TURNS

The "Battle of the Atlantic" was on the verge of dramatic reversal initiated by a series of Allied scientific accomplishments. In the United States, the Harvard Underwater Sound Laboratory developed improvements over the British ASDIC and named the new system of sound detection SONAR (Sound Navigation and Ranging). In addition, the Allies equipped their airplanes with radar, extremely powerful searchlights, and massive 1,000 pound depth charges. Earlier planes carried only 100 pound bombs that were totally unsuited for anti-submarine action. Considering those earlier Allied efforts, Dönitz had reflected, "An aircraft can no more kill a U-boat than a crow can kill a mole." But what was true then no longer applied. Airplanes were now equipped to strike deadly blows and U-boats could no longer run on the surface under the cover of darkness in relative safety.

"Unterseeboots" was a popular misnomer for German World War II submarines that, like those of other navies, were actually surface craft that could remain submerged for only short periods. They were forced to surface frequently for charging batteries and ventilation. They submerged only to evade the enemy or to attack. They might more properly have been called "diving boats."

Dönitz' counter to the air offense was to order U-boats to hunt in packs within the 600 mile mid-Atlantic "Air Gap," an area out of reach of shore-based aircraft. The Allies countered by adding escort carriers to their convoys. Another action to close the net on marauding U-boats was to introduce Hunter-Killer Groups, usually consisting of four escort destroyers and a Jeep Aircraft Carrier converted from a merchant ship. Roaming the Atlantic in search of U-boats, these groups created the effect of mobile air bases all over the Atlantic. There was no place for U-boats to hide; there were no more "mid-ocean gaps," and a German submarine could be attacked by aircraft anywhere at sea. Before the end of the war, 47% of all U-boat sinkings would be attributed to Allied aircraft, a far cry from the relatively ineffectual role of the airplane in World War I anti-submarine action.

An unidentified U-boat under aerial attack from an American aircraft. Note the S shaped wake as the U-boat tries to evade the attacking plane. Courtesy of National Archives.

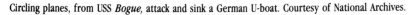

Circling planes, from USS *Bogue,* attack and sink a German U-boat. Courtesy of National Archives.

An American PBM Mariner flying boat drops a stick of four bombs on a U-boat in the South Atlantic in May 1943. Courtesy of National Archives.

U-boat under aerial attack. Courtesy of National Archives.

Another decisive factor to alter the balance of power was the perfection of high-frequency, direction-finding techniques that allowed destroyer escorts to lock in on even short duration radio transmissions. Throughout the war, the U-boat High Command insisted on frequent weather and patrol data transmissions from its boats at sea that would in turn receive convoy position information and changes in orders. Each such transmission offered an opportunity for attack by one of the newly equipped destroyer escorts.

Further, improved weapons were developed for the destruction of submerged U-boats. One was the Hedgehog, which eliminated the need for an attacking destroyer to pass over a diving submarine to release its depth charges. The Hedgehog provided a pattern of 24 rocket-launched projectiles which could be fired from the bow of an attacking vessel at the site of a diving U-boat. The projectiles exploded only on contact, permitting the attack vessel to maintain constant sonar contact with an elusive target victim.

Hedgehog projectiles being loaded on spigots. Courtesy of National Archives.

The Hedgehog was a multi-spigot mortar that launched a salvo of 24 30-pound charges of high explosive 250 yards ahead of the vessel carrying it. They landed in a circular pattern and exploded only on contact. This new development allowed attacking escort vessels to maintain sonar contact with the target. Courtesy of National Archives.

Germany's Enigma code machine was invented by a Dutchman Hugo Knoch, in 1919. It looked like a typewriter and contained a series of drums that could be selected for a prescribed pattern to encode and decode messages. The German armed forces believed the code machine to be foolproof and were unaware that the British had obtained one. During the war nearly all Enigma messages were deciphered by the British who code-named these intercepts Ultra. Courtesy of National Archives.

A major factor in the growing success of the Allies over the U-boat was an early intelligence breakthrough that was accomplished with the cooperation of the Polish Secret Service. In 1939, one of Germany's Enigma code machines was stolen from the plant where it was produced. In a master stroke of espionage, the machine was transported to England, where the Government Code and Cypher School devoted its full energies to the problem until the code was broken. With the information thus made available by intercepted German transmissions, convoys were rerouted around U-boat patrol lines. The combination of intelligence penetration and technological developments turned the tide against the German underwater fleet and sealed the fate of Germany in World War II. The U-boat had suddenly become vulnerable, and obsolescent.

The sudden turn of events was dramatic in the speed with which it was accomplished. In March 1943, German wolf-packs had won a fierce battle against an Allied convoy, sinking twenty-one ships while losing only one U-boat. Less than two months later, in early May, another wolf-pack sank nine ships of a convoy, but in the process, 11 of its 12 attackers were lost to the escort vessels. A few days after that, a five-boat pack was totally destroyed while sinking only five ships.

Close to the end of the same month, escort vessels of another convoy sank six U-boats without losing a ship. The impact of that action was particularly heavy on Germany's Admiral Dönitz. His son Peter was lost aboard *U-954*.

Germany's hopes waned as, from mid-1943 through to the end of the war, the German loss ratio remained at more than one U-boat to one Allied ship. On December 14, 1943, Dönitz wrote:

> For months past the enemy has rendered the U-boat ineffective. He has achieved this object not through superior tactics or strategy but through his superiority in the field of science; this finds its expression in the modern battle weapon — detection. By this means he had torn our sole offensive weapon in the war against the Anglo-Saxons from our hands.

A depth charge explosion off the stern creates a mountainous geyser as the U.S. Coast Guard cutter *Spencer* attacks *U-175* on April 7, 1943. Convoy can be seen in the distance. The U-boat was forced to the surface; then she was scuttled by her crew. Courtesy of National Archives.

A German submariner, one of 41 survivors of *U-175* calls for assistance moments after the badly damaged U-boat was scuttled. Courtesy of National Archives.

Despite the shocking losses in U-boats and their crews, Hitler ordered Dönitz to continue the battle. Huge Allied naval forces were being tied up by the U-boats and the bombing efforts on German cities was reduced. Dönitz summed up the situation:

> If we stopped sending out U-boats the enemy would stop escorting his convoys. As it is, we know that our U-boats are pinning down about two million enemy personnel in warships and in repair shops, quite apart from the time he loses through having to operate the convoy system at all. So we must keep our U-boats at sea even if they never sink a ship. Their mere presence alone constitutes a success for us.

Such information did little to improve the morale of U-boat crews, faced with the reality that they no longer represented their country's offensive threat; they were merely a sacrificial diversion.

SUPER U-BOAT

Dönitz knew, as he sat in conference with the Führer in September 1942, that the "Battle of the Atlantic" was lost unless more formidable U-boats could be put to sea, and soon. His prized U-boat fleet was fast becoming obsolete. Dr. Hellmuth Walter, a brilliant German submarine engineer, had already designed a truly underwater vessel that could provide the answer. It was capable of remainiug submerged for long periods,

operated underwater at high speed, and was designed to dive deeper than any before her.

Dr. Walter had experimented before the war with a turbine engine fueled by a concentration of hydrogen-peroxide called Perhydrol. The turbine required no air for combustion and released heat for propulsion plus water vapor and oxygen as beneficent by-products.

In his desperate need for a new U-boat, Dönitz was emboldened to press Hitler for approval to immediately mass-produce a larger version of Walter's latest experimental vessel, the Type XVII. It would be the 1,600 ton Type XVIII, powered by the Walter turbine. Hitler agreed.

Almost immediately, it was evident that, despite the Führer's support, the priority demands of rocket missiles and Luftwaffe aircraft for Perhydrol would cripple Walter turbine U-boats for lack of fuel.

It was decided to abandon the Type XVIII, but the streamlined hull of the Walter boat would be retained in the innovative design of the new, Type XXI "Elektroboot" (Electric Boat). Walter's Type XVIII pressure hull had been structured like an inverted figure 8 with the smaller circle at the bottom to store the massive amounts of Perhydrol fuel required. That planned fuel storage area was ideal for housing the array of storage batteries needed to power the Type XXI. They were to provide for submerged propulsion while light-weight diesel engines were to be used on the surface. The new U-boat was indeed a submarine, designed to operate almost entirely below the surface, at great depths, and at high speed. Her range of 11,000 miles, new air purification system, submerged speed of 17 knots, and schnorchel depth speed of 12 knots, twice as fast as earlier types, justified the term "Wonder Boat." Unfortunately for the German war effort, only two of them entered service before the war ended.

UNITED STATES ENTRY

As a neutral, the United States had been assisting Great Britain by shipping huge quantities of war materials across the Atlantic and providing naval support to escort cargo vessels. So many encounters occurred in the eastern Atlantic between American vessels and German U-boats that undeclared warfare on the high seas was recognized by both nations. On October 10, 1941, a U-boat torpedoed the U.S. destroyer *Kearney* while it was on escort duty. *Kearney* lost 11 of her crew but did not sink. However, 21 days later, another U-boat sent the U.S. destroyer *Reuben James* to the bottom. With that sinking, the United States had lost her first warship in the "Battle of the Atlantic." But not even that disaster precipitated a declaration of war against Germany. The United States was still officially neutral.

Germany's ally, Japan, struck Pearl Harbor on the morning of December 7, 1941 and Congress declared war the next day. Germany declared war on December 11. The Japanese attack may have been a surprise to the German High Command, but official entry of the United States into World War II stimulated immediate response from the U-boat High Command. German military strategists reasoned that a stranglehold on the flow of men and supplies from America was essential for victory in Europe. The means to that objective was clearly the German Navy's fleet of U-boats.

The opportunity to attack shipping in American waters provided an inviting prospect to U-boat commanders. United States coastal defenses were inexperienced in anti-submarine warfare. Months would be required to organize defenses and to group merchant ships into protective convoys under naval and air escort.

The optimism of the U-boat commanders was well-founded. Merchant ships sailed with normal peacetime lighting and coastal cities, brightly illuminated, offered a silhouette of passing ships to prowling U-boats. Lighthouses and buoys continued to display invaluable navigational information. U-boat commanders intercepted uncoded communications concerning speed, course, and position between merchant ships and shore as well as radio details of destroyer sailings and aircraft patrols.

Operation "Paukenschlag" (Drumbeat) was Germany's initial blow against America's eastern seaboard. Between December 16 and 25, Dönitz ordered five U-boats, all he had available at the time, to American waters between the St. Lawrence and Cape Hatteras. Ninety-one U-boats were operational, but 23 were not available because they were in the Mediterranean, blocked off from reaching the Atlantic. The rest were involved in other operations or in dockyards for repair.

The five German U-boats wrought havoc on unsuspecting American merchantmen. The slaughter proved again that its U-boat fleet was the German Navy's most telling combat arm. During the day, the U-boats rested safely on the bottom. At night, they surfaced to take their toll of ships silhouetted against a brilliantly lighted coastline. They were safe from air attack because the United States Navy had only 125 planes — and they could not be used at night. A feeble force of about 20 obsolete destroyers and 34 English patrol boats, hastily dispatched by the British Admiralty, were the only anti-submarine surface vessels available to patrol the thousands of miles of brightly illuminated coast. Without experience and poorly organized, those token anti-submarine forces were useless against the U-boat onslaught.

"Paukenschlag" netted 25 ships totalling about 200,000 tons in the first ten days. Many of those were tankers — a severe blow to the Allied war effort. Korvettenkapitän Hardegen *(U-123)* sank eight ships, 53,360 tons, including three tankers; Korvettenkapitän Zapp *(U-66)* sank five ships, 50,000 tons, two of which were tankers; Korvettenkapitän Kals *(U-130)* sank four ships, 30,748 tons, three of them tankers. The two other boats accounted for eight ships for about 65,000 tons between them. All five of the U-boats were the large Type IX, designed for long range operation.

Before the first five U-boats left the operational area, three more large U-boats arrived off Chesapeake Bay to continue the one-sided conflict. All available long range U-boats were by then deployed, so the next group sent to American waters consisted solely of the medium size Type VII. They had been used largely against convoys, where high speed was essential — without concern for fuel consumption or operating range. During Atlantic crossings, the Captains and Chief Engineers of those smaller U-boats experimented with measures to conserve fuel. As an example, while winter gales were blowing, a U-boat would travel submerged, with little loss of speed, course

The torpedoed tanker *Bryon D. Benson,* victim of Erich Topp in *U-552* flames out of control off Cape Hatteras on April 5, 1942. Courtesy of National Archives.

Black smoke billows from the torpedoed tanker *Dixie Arrow,* carrying 88,000 barrels of crude oil, off Cape Hatteras, a favored hunting ground for U-boats, in March 1942. Courtesy of National Archives.

The Standard Oil Company tanker *R. P. Resor,* 7,451 tons, torpedoed by *U-578* on February 26, 1942, off New Jersey. Only two members of the 49-man crew were rescued. The tanker's cargo of 105,025 barrels of crude oil fed the raging fires, and the billowing clouds of smoke could easily be seen from shore. *R. P. Resor* sank the following day in 100 feet of water, 32 miles off Barnegat, New Jersey. Courtesy of Submarine Force Library and Museum.

Another U-boat victim, *Tiger,* begins to settle by the stern after being torpedoed by *U-754* off Norfolk, Virginia on April 2, 1942. Courtesy of National Archives.

unimpeded by the storm, and precious fuel conserved. Crews willingly sacrificed personal amenities to accommodate additional stores and extra fuel. Fresh water tanks were loaded with fuel at the sacrifice of drinking water and washing supply. By such means, a Type VII U-boat could arrive in American waters with about 20 tons of fuel, enough to remain on patrol for two to three weeks.

Dönitz' campaign against American shipping received a severe blow near the end of January, 1942 — not from the Allies, but from his own Führer. Hitler experienced an intuitive warning. He envisioned an Allied invasion of Norway and ordered Dönitz to dispatch all available U-boats to Norwegian waters to repel the enemy. Dönitz complied in part, but he continued to send a few U-boats to American waters. The effect of Hitler's interference was that there were never more than eight U-boats operating in the Western Atlantic at one time. Though they were few in number, their impact was astounding.

Hardegen *(U-123)* returned to the American "shooting gallery" in mid-March 1942, and sank 11 ships. Korvettenkapitän Mohr *(U-124)* sent nine ships to the bottom. Korvettenkapitän Lassen *(U-160)*, Korvettenkapitän Muzelburg *(U-203)*, and Korvettenkapitän Topp *(U-552)* each claimed to have sunk at least five Allied vessels. Elated over the success of his mission in American waters, Jochen Mohr *(U-124)* tried his hand at poetry with the following:

> The new moon night is black as ink
> Off Hatteras the tankers sink
> While sadly Roosevelt counts the score
> Some fifty thousand tons — by Mohr

Mohr's success off Cape Hatteras boosted his sinkings to over 100,000 tons. His crew aboard *U-124* realized that he would be awarded the Knight's Cross for that achievement. One of the crewmen, Mechanikermaat Loba, created a replica of the decoration in anticipation of the award announcement by radio. When it was received, the message was withheld from Mohr until the cook had baked a cake decorated in icing with the coveted award. With all in readiness, the crew woke the captain from a sound sleep with the call "Commander to the Bridge!" Congratulations greeted him, and he was presented with the facsimile Knight's Cross and cake. Later, he was awarded the decoration by Admiral Dönitz, but for the remainder of his life, he would wear only the one his men had made for him. That would be only one year. On April 2, 1943, British warships sank *U-124*, with the loss of all hands, including Korvettenkapitän Mohr.

Their successes in U.S. waters startled even the most optimistic of the U-boat commanders. In January 1942, 35 ships were sunk, 45 in February, and 76 in March. April showed a drop to 52, but in May the total was 105 and in June, 110. During the first half of 1942, U-boats claimed 423 merchant ships sunk in the western Atlantic. By mid-1942, American defenses had managed to sink several U-boats off the American coast, but that was very small consolation for the wholesale losses of Allied merchant shipping.

By July 1942, American cities had doused their lights, radio communication was controlled, and the convoy system was in operation along the east coast. Those once lucrative waters were no longer easy pickings for the U-boat. There, as elsewhere in the war theater, Allied counter-action had wrested the initiative from the U-boat, reversing her role from hunter to prey. The once happy days of sea domination and shooting gallery sinkings, measured in millions of tons, had come to an end.

WAR ENDS

The Allies invaded France on June 6, 1944, and by the start of 1945 it was apparent that Germany could not hold out much longer. As the year progressed, city after city in Germany capitulated. The Allied front advanced as rapidly from the west as the Russians did from the east. The worst fears of Germany had materialized — she was trapped in the middle and the end was obvious. On May 1, the suicide of Hitler was announced and Admiral Dönitz was the new head of the German state. At 2:41 A.M. on May 7, German Chief of Staff, General Alfred Jodl and Admiral Georg Friedeburg, Dönitz' replacement commanding the German Navy, signed the Act of Military Surrender at a small red schoolhouse in Reims, France. The following day formal surrender papers were signed at Berlin, terms becoming effective at 12:01 A.M. European time on May 9.

With the capitulation of Germany, pressure mounted against Japan in the Pacific. On August 6, 1945, the city of Hiroshima was atomic bombed, followed three days later by another atomic bombing, on the Japanese city of Nagasaki. The devastating effect of those attacks forced the capitualtion of Japan. Formal surrender documents were signed on September 2, aboard the American battleship *Missouri* anchored in Tokyo Bay. After six years of conflict, World War II came to an end.

During the first World War, Germany's U-boats were neutralized, but during the second war they were defeated. The U-boats of World War II

Gustav Krupp, son-in-law of Freidrich Alfred Krupp, builder of the Kaiser's pre-World War I navy. Gustav was implicated at Nuremberg after World War II in the plotting of Nazi aggression and secret rearmament of the Reich. However, medical authorities unanimously agreed the 75-year-old industrialist would never be in a physical or mental state to appear before the court. He died five years later. His son Alfried, member of the SS, was convicted and sentenced to imprisonment for 12 years. The conviction was not for his SS role, but because of the part he had played in the spoliation of other countries and the exploitation and maltreatment of large masses of forced foreign labor to achieve Hitler's objectives. Courtesy of National Archives.

created a legend, but at a fearful penalty. They sank 148 Allied warships and destroyed 2,779 merchant ships for a total of 14,119,413 gross tons. The price they paid was 784 U-boats lost of 1,150 commissioned; of 40,000 crewmen, 28,000 died and 5,000 were captured. Such are the terrible statistics of war.

This book explores the legends, myths, and truths of U-boats sunk in American waters that are shallow enough to be visited by amateur scuba divers. It sets the backdrop against which sport divers can appreciate the underwater museum they are visiting — a museum of historical significance that they are privileged to enjoy, and are obliged to respect during their brief dive into history.

PART II

THE U-BOATS

CHAPTER FOUR

VICTOR'S PRIZE — UC-97

UC-97 was not one of Germany's glamour U-boats. She had no war record and nothing to distinguish her from the rest of World War I's German Imperial Navy except that she was viewed and toured and touched by thousands of American prospects for Victory Bonds after the war. Her history is mundane and colorless, but her possible accessibility for scuba diving warrants including the U-boat in this *Dive Into History.*

This U-boat was designed to lay mines but the war ended before she could be placed in service. Mine-layers were recognized to be essential to the German war effort as the most effective means of hampering the flow of supplies, ordnance, and troops to and from Great Britain, particularly through the English Channel. Unless that flow could be choked off, the Kaiser's dream of victory would never be realized. With nearby Belgian and French ports available to them, German military strategists concluded that the most effective naval action would be to infest the waters between England and France with contact mines. However, constant Allied monitoring of the Channel demanded that mine placement be performed quietly without attracting the attention of observant enemy lookouts. A small, short-range U-boat was the answer.

UCI SERIES

Early in 1915, Germany introduced a new, 168-ton mine-laying U-boat, only 111.5 feet long. Six vertical shafts installed in the bow were designed to release mines through the keel. In order to maintain trim and keep the boat from popping to the surface, compensating water ballast was taken on each time a mine was dropped. The design was effective and the new U-boats proved their ability to escape detection. The consternation of mystified British naval circles during the summer of 1915 was adequate evidence. The growing numbers of merchant ships damaged without report of enemy vessels in the vicinity left only the unpleasant possibility that enemy warships disguised as neutrals were responsible. That suspicion prevailed until July, 1915. Then, by accident, the truth unfolded. A steamship, passing off the coast of Yarmouth, England, reported striking a submerged object. No surface evidence of the collision was observed and the incident might have passed without further investigation except that the area was rocked by an explosion that night, hours after the accident. The next morning, Navy divers discovered the wreckage of a small German mine-layer, *UC-2.* One of her mines had apparently detonated as the sunken U-boat lay on the bottom. The British Admiralty understood the nature of the threat with that revelation, but more was to come.

The following April, another small mine-layer, *UC-5* ran aground on the east coast of England. Her commander conscientiously followed his standing instructions to destroy signal books and charts. Fortunately for the British, the demolition charges failed to explode before a British destroyer arrived. The U-boat was towed to Harwich for examination by British technical experts and intelligence officers. The first German U-boat to fall into British hands provided insight into submarine development, contact mine technology, and signal codes of the German Navy. The knowledge helped but mine-laying continued to harass Allied shipping.

UC-5 ran aground and was captured by the British in April 1916. She was exhibited in various English ports. This postcard illustration shows the manner in which mines were dropped through the keel. Water ballast was admitted to compensate for weight loss, which otherwise would have caused the U-boat to rise to the required surface. The same mine-laying system was used on *UC-97*. Source: (British) Ministry of Defence Navy Department.

UCII SERIES

Germany followed with the larger UCII series in 1916 and the even larger UCIII in 1917. Their increased size accommodated more mines and extended their range of operations. UCI armament consisted of a single machine gun. An 86mm deck gun was added to the UCII series which was also fitted with torpedo tubes. Explicit instructions were issued that torpedoes were to be fired only after the U-boat had shed her dangerous cargo of mines. The stern torpedo tube was mounted internally and could be reloaded underway, as in other U-boats. The two forward tubes, however, were external because the forward mine shafts left no space inside the pressure hull. Once fired, the forward tubes could not be reloaded until the U-boat returned to her base.

The diving qualities of UCII boats fell short of expectations. In addition, when underway on the surface, spray from the forward deck gun and external torpedo tubes inundated the deck gun platform and conning tower. The wet bridge condition was dangerous and exceedingly unpleasant, especially during winter months.

UCIII SERIES

The UCIII added spare torpedoes, stored externally, but the U-boat had to surface in order to gain access to them. UCIII was also more heavily armed with a larger 105mm deck gun. To compensate for her increased armament, the UCIII carried only 14 mines compared to the 18 carried by UCII.

A new hull shape was designed to correct the spray condition. The streamlined UCIII carried a raked "shark-nose" bow with a net cutter and a deck that sloped gently down from bow to conning tower. The forward torpedo tubes, cause of most of the spray, were relocated abreast the conning tower and the deck gun was raised.

The changes did nothing to improve diving time, but they did correct the water spray problem. However, when the U-boat was underway a stream of foam, clearly visible to the enemy, formed around the torpedo tubes. Germany's series of mine-laying U-boats were highly advanced but still short of perfection.

WAR ENDS

UC-97, the subject of this chapter, was one of that UCIII series. She was laid down late in 1917 by Blohm & Voss at Hamburg, Germany and was launched March 17, 1918, but never commissioned. The Armistice that ended hostilities in November, before the U-boat had completed her trials, included the following surrender provisions:

> To surrender at the ports specified by the Allies and the United States all submarines at present in existence (including all submarine-cruisers and mine-layers), with armament and equipment complete.

Harwich, the British port where the grounded mine-layer, *UC-5* was so carefully examined by technicians and intelligence experts in 1916, was named as the port of surrender for 176 U-boats.

Forward 105mm (4.1 inch) deck gun of *UC-97*. U-boats sank most of their victims with gunfire during the First World War to save precious torpedoes. Torpedoes and fuel supply determined how long a U-boat could spend on patrol. Courtesy of U.S. Naval Historical Center.

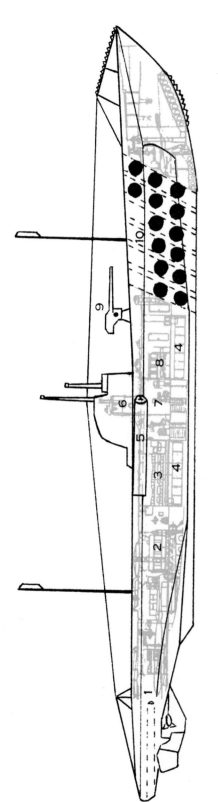

TYPE UCIII

1. Aft torpedo room
2. Engine room
3. Crew quarters
4. Batteries
5. Amidship torpedo tube

6. Conning tower
7. Control room
8. Officer's quarters
9. 105mm deck gun
10. Mine chutes with mines

Displacement (tons)
Surfaced 491
Submerged 571
Length.. 185'4"
Beam .... 18'3"
Draught .... 12'6"
Speed (knots)
Surfaced 11.5
Submerged 6.6
Range (nautical miles/kn.)
Surfaced 8,200/7
Submerged 40/4.5
Armament
Amidship torpedo tubes 2
Stern torpedo tubes 1
Torpedoes carried (number/size) .... 7/19.7"
Mine chutes 6
Mines carried 14
Guns (number/size)... 1/105mm
Crew.. 32

Surrendered World War I U-boats at Harwich, England, after the Armistice in 1918. During the war 178 were sunk and 176 surrendered at Harwich. Courtesy of National Archives.

Twenty miles out of port, British crews boarded the German vessels and hoisted the White Ensign above the German flag. German commanding officers were spared that humiliation of surrender through the use of special crews that had been engaged to navigate the U-boats into the hands of the British.

The prominent net-cutter on *UC-97's* bow creates the impression of shark's teeth in this post-WWI photograph. The photo caption *UC-7* is incorrect. *UC-7* sank in July, 1916 — the first submarine to be sunk by a depth charge. Courtesy of U. S. Naval Historical Center.

The United States expressed interest in obtaining several of the surrendered submarines for technical study and for use as exhibits in a Victory Bond drive in the United States. That request was granted early in 1919, with the stipulation that the vessels would be destroyed after they had served the purposes for which they had been approved. *UC-97* and five other U-boats were allocated to the United States. The other five boats, *U-111, U-117, U-140, UB-88,* and *UB-148* were eventually sunk in water too deep for divers to visit with conventional scuba gear (see Appendix G). Six experienced commanders, six executive officers, and 120 enlisted men left the United States in March, 1919 to ferry the U-boats across the Atlantic from England. Lt. Commander Holbrook Gibson was assigned command of *UC-97,* with Lt. Commander Charles Lockwood as his executive officer.

SABOTAGE

What might have been a simple ferrying operation was severely complicated by the American crew's unfamiliarity with diesel engines and the German language compounded by the clever sabotage of their vessels by the U-boat crews who brought the war prizes to the point of surrender. *U-111,* for example, had been delivered to England with her bearings intentionally burned out. The last hour of her voyage had been carefully calculated to ensure that she would arrive in England — but barely. Her starboard engine oil valves were completely closed.

April 3 was set as the date of departure from England for the six U-boats. Two of them, *U-111* and *U-140,* could not be readied in time for departure, a tribute to the inspired sabotage program of the German crews. As the hour of departure approached, it was feared that *UC-97* would also have to be left behind. Her diesel engines were out of operation but the American crew was confident that the problem could be corrected while the U-boat was at sea. It was decided that the submarine tender, *Bushnell* would take *UC-97* in tow to get the small flotilla underway. By late afternoon of the first day, the confidence of the American crew was rewarded as *UC-97*'s engines roared into action. The tow line was dropped and the U-boat completed the rest of the crossing under her own power.

American officers on board a German U-boat war prize in Harwich, England, one of six allocated to the United States for study and promotional purposes after the end of World War I. Courtesy of National Archives.

USS *Bushnell*, "Mother Ship" to the small flotilla of World War I U-boats that were allocated to the United States, was named after David Bushnell who built a submarine in 1775. Bushnell's submarine was used in an unsuccessful attack on British warships in New York Harbor. Courtesy of U. S. Naval Historical Center.

War prize *UC-97* entering New York Harbor under the watchful eyes of the Statue of Liberty. One of the two external torpedo tubes can be seen abreast of the conning tower. Courtesy of U.S. Navy.

Services were held aboard *UC-97* on May 8, 1919, marking the anniversary of the sinking of *Lusitania.* The British liner was sunk off the coast of Ireland on May 7, 1915, with the loss of 1,198 lives, of which 124 were American. A large wreath was thrown overboard by the Victory Bond Committee. Courtesy of U.S. Navy.

AMERICAN TOUR

The strange German-American naval armada was referred to as the even stranger "Ex-German Submarine Expeditionary Force." The five vessels headed from England to the Azores, then to Bermuda. Out of Bermuda, *Bushnell* and her four U-boats set course for New York City, where they arrived 24 days out of Harwich, England. After arrival, the U-boats were opened to the public. Reporters, photographers, tourists, naval technicians, and civilian boat builders covered every

inch of them. Then the U-boats were separated, each to cover a region of the United States in the interest of the Government's Victory Bond campaign. *UC-97* was assigned to the Great Lakes region. That required her to pass through the locks of the Canadian-controlled St. Lawrence canal system. Canadian protocol called for vessels to fly the Union Jack at the fore. *UC-97*'s American captain, former Executive Officer Lt. Commander Charles A. Lockwood, Jr., refused claiming rights as a war vessel. He refused to

Starboard view of *U-111*'s bridge. Photo was taken at the Philadelphia Navy Yard in 1920. Courtesy of National Archives.

One of Germany's surrendered U-boats, draped with a U.S. flag, on a float for a Victory Bond parade in the United States. A nurse, by the submarine's rudder, waves another U.S. flag. Courtesy Submarine Force Library and Museum.

Visitors aboard *U-117* in Washington, D.C. She was a Type UEII ocean mine-layer. During the war *U-117* made one war patrol to American waters and sank 23 vessels for 35,000 tons. Unlike the coastal mine-layers of the UC Type, UEII's received a U-number designation. Courtesy of National Archives.

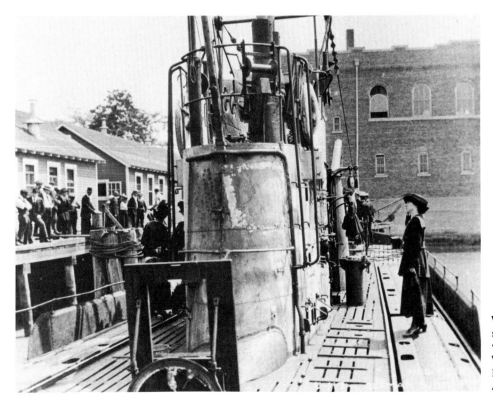

Woman visitor inspects starboard side of *U-117* conning tower while the U-boat is on display in Washington, D.C., for Victory Bond Drive. Courtesy of National Archives.

budge from that position despite trouble at each Canadian port of call. Lockwood, who later rose to fame in World War II as Vice Admiral, Commander, Submarines, Pacific Fleet, stuck to his position and was later vindicated by Canadian naval officers who supported his dedicated adherence to naval tradition.

A series of visits to large and small American ports on Lakes Ontario, Erie, Huron, and Michigan followed. Plans to continue through Lake Superior were cancelled when the U-boat's engines showed signs of fatigue. In August, she headed for Chicago and before the end of the month, UC-97 was turned over to the Commandant, 9th Naval District. She remained at the Great Lakes Naval Station until June 7, 1921. Then, in accordance with the agreement that she would be destroyed, the U-boat was taken out into Lake Michigan and sunk by USS Wilmette in a naval reserve gunnery drill. After 18 rounds of 4" shells had been fired, the U-boat went to the bottom.

FRESH WATER GRAVE

The deck log of Wilmette reports the location of the sinking at 42°10' N, 87°20' W, an area of Lake Michigan that is approximately 20 miles east of Highland Park, Illinois. The depth at that point is between 204 and 252 feet. However, Harry Cooper, president of Sharkhunters, an organization dedicated to finding and preserving the history and artifacts of U-boats, has a depth recorder printout that shows what he feels is UC-97 in 110 feet of water.

The fresh water conditions are ideal to preserve her far longer than those U-boats that have been sunk in salt water off the Eastern Seaboard. It would be a boon to interested scuba divers to provide them with the precise location of the German vessel. Unfortunately, the exact location is not known, except perhaps to Harry Cooper. Many other researchers have looked for UC-97, but apparently she maintained neutral bouyancy as she drifted beneath the surface rather than dropping straight to the bottom. Perhaps a reader, stimulated by this account, will conduct further, more productive research. Or the symbol of World War I naval history may be discovered by the random pattern of a passing vessel's depth recording. Then, at least in the exciting world of scuba, German mine-layer UC-97 will command the attention and respect she merits as an historic site that she was denied as a potentially lethal weapon of the War for Democracy, World War I.

UC-97 and UB-88 under study at the Brooklyn Navy Yard. The small Type UB submarines were developed for coastal operations. Courtesy of U.S. Naval Historical Center.

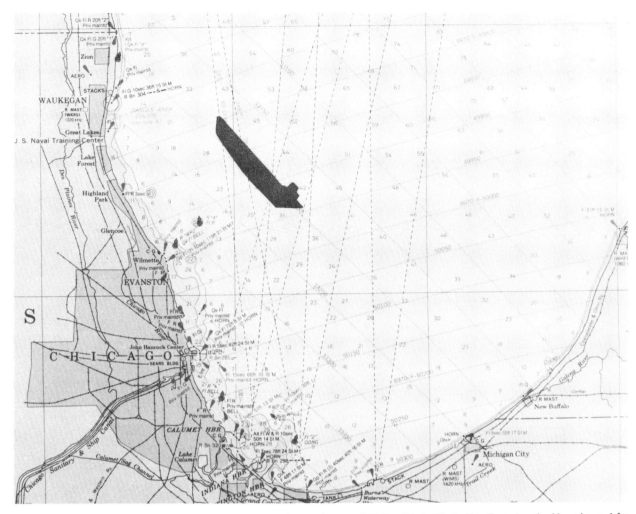

UC-97 was reportedly sunk at 42° 10′ N, 87° 20′ W, approximately 20 miles east of Highland Park, Illinois. This illustration should not be used for navigational purposes.

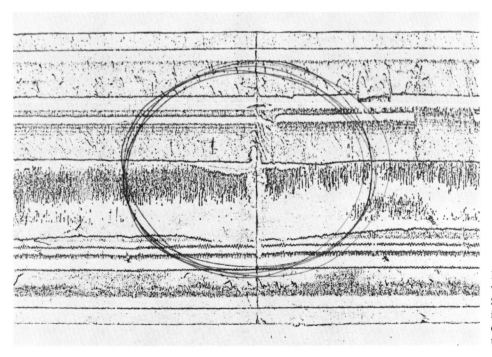

Depth recorder printout shows what Harry Cooper, president of Sharkhunters, believes is *UC-97* in 110 feet of water. Indeed, it does look like a submarine. Courtesy of Harry Cooper.

CHAPTER FIVE

WRONG PLACE — WRONG TIME — U-85

One of the most decisive military conflicts in the history of warfare was termed by Winston Churchill, the "Battle of the Atlantic," the confrontation that pitted Germany's World War II submarine fleet against Britain, Canada, and the United States. He wrote in *The Second World War:*

> The only thing that ever really frightened me during the war was the U-boat peril . . . I was even more anxious about this battle than I had been about the glorious air fight called the 'Battle of Britain.'

The struggle for control of the Atlantic actually began in World War I, during which German U-boats sank more than 5,000 Allied ships. During the period between the two wars, Allied naval planners were lulled into complacency. They were convinced that the convoy system, equipped with improved anti-submarine devices could control the undersea menace of Germany's U-boats. It had eventually done so before the end of World War I. How wrong they were is evidenced by the conjecture of reputable historians who believe that only 50 more U-boats, at the beginning, might have won the war for Germany. They acknowledge that wars are not won exclusively by freighters and tankers, but wars can be lost without them. Churchill wrote in *The Second World War:*

> Battles might be won or lost, enterprises succeed or miscarry, territories might be gained or quitted, but dominating all our power to carry on the war, or even keep ourselves alive, was our mastery of the ocean routes and the free approach and entry to our ports.

Britains mastery of the seas was truly the challenge confronting Germany. At the outbreak of World War II, Germany's main operational U-boat, Type VII, had an operating radius of 4,300 miles at a speed of 12 knots. *U-85* was one of 24 Type VIIB's with an increased operating range of 6,500 miles at 12 knots and 8,700 miles at 10 knots. The new model was larger than the Type VII and carried modified external saddle tanks to increase fuel capacity. Higher performance diesel engines produced a surface speed of 17.25 knots. Submerged, the VIIB was limited to 8 knots, the same as her predecessor, VIIA. As a measure to increase the striking power of the VIIB, pressure-tight containers were installed on the deck to house two reserve torpedoes. Another was stowed in the stern torpedo compartment, increasing the number of torpedoes carried from 11 to 14.

The first VIIB went into service in June, 1938. One, *U-48,* gained distinction by sinking the highest tonnage of enemy shipping in World War II — 51 ships for a total of 310,400 tons. Her commander, Herbert Schultze, is less well known for his compassionate action in radioing the Admiralty in London to send rescue for the survivors of a ship he had just sunk.

THE U-BOAT

U-85 was commissioned on June 7, 1941, under the command of Oberleutnant zur See Eberhard Greger, a six-year veteran from the naval class of 1935. The new U-boat was constructed by Flender Werft at Lubeck, Germany. She measured 218'3" long, 20'3" beam and displaced 753 tons. For five weeks, she performed in the Baltic for the

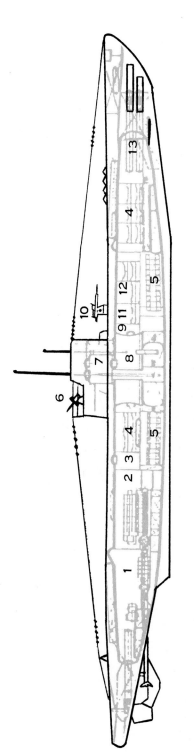

TYPE VIIB

1. Aft torpedo room & electric motor
2. Diesel engine room
3. Galley
4. Crew quarters
5. Batteries
6. 20mm anti-aircraft gun
7. Conning tower
8. Control room
9. Radio room
10. 88mm deck gun
11. Commander's quarters
12. Officer's quarters
13. Forward torpedo room

Displacement (tons)
Surfaced 753
Submerged 857
Length . . . . 218'3"
Beam . . . . 20'3"
Draught . . . . 15'6"
Fuel capacity (tons) 108
Speed (knots)
Surfaced 17.25
Submerged 8
Range (nautical miles/kn.)
Surfaced 8,100/10
Submerged 90/4
Armament
Bow torpedo tubes 4
Stern torpedo tubes 1
Torpedoes carried (number/size) . . . . 14/21"
Guns (number/size) . . . . 1/20mm — 1/88mm
Crew 44

The Kriegsmarine ensign flutters above *U-85* crewmen as they relax on deck for relief from the humidity and odors of the interior. Courtesy U.S. Naval Historical Center.

U-boat Acceptance Commission. After check-out tests were completed, *U-85* joined a group of U-boats for tactical exercises. Then, in mid-July, she returned to Lubeck, her crew eager for combat. However, another six weeks would pass before she embarked on her first war cruise. During that period, *U-85* was rammed by the German destroyer *T-151* in an accident during gunnery practice drills off the coast of Norway. Her number one ballast tank and steering gear were damaged. The fledgling U-boat had absorbed the first punishment of a career that was to endure only a short ten months.

FIRST WAR CRUISE

U-85 left Trondheim, Norway for her first war cruise, her conning tower proudly adorned with a painted symbol of the sleek fighting machine — a wild boar with a white rose clenched in his teeth. An incongruous dichotomy of savage efficiency and delicate purity, *U-85* headed for her first mission.

A freighter was sighted on the third day out, but it escaped while the U-boat was trying to maneuver into firing position. Another, sighted a day later, proved to be an escort vessel of only 300 to 400 tons — not worth a torpedo. Six days out, *U-85* barely escaped a three-depth-charge air attack despite a constant air watch. From then on, lookouts were even more attentive to the threat from the sky.

On September 9, en route to her station at the northern end of a seven-U-boat patrol code-named "Markgraf," *U-85* ran into unbelievable luck. The patrol was stretched over the sea lanes between Greenland and Iceland, combing the sea in search of Allied eastbound convoys. By chance, but a tribute to the vigilance of her look-out, *U-85* sighted the smoke of a slow, east-bound, 70 ship Canadian convoy, SC-42, escorted by a destroyer and three corvettes. The find was radioed to U-boat Headquarters and the "Markgraf" group was ordered to concentrate on *U-85*'s convoy.

Eight ships were torpedoed that night and three more the next morning despite desperate evasive action by the slow merchant ships. At one point, *U-85* headed for a promising plume of smoke but was forced under by enemy aircraft. Later, five torpedoes were fired — without a hit. The chagrined crew attributed the multiple miss, not to their own inaccuracy or evasive action by the intended victim but to defective torpedoes. That was the opening of a 37-hour engagement during which *U-85* was forced to submerge nine times by air alarms or enemy warships. Kept abreast of the attack by radio, Admiral Dönitz ordered, "This

convoy must not get through. U-boats PURSUE, ATTACK, AND SINK." Before the action was disengaged, 16 ships of the convoy were sunk, a brilliant victory for Germany's underwater fleet. During the attack, *U-85* fired nine torpedoes at four ships over a 33-hour pursuit. Eight hours after the start, Oberleutnant Greger focused attention on two vessels, the nearer an escort, the more distant a freighter stopped dead in the water. It was a classic U-boat trap in Greger's estimation. He decided not to accept the challenge and submerged. An hour later, he re-surfaced, still in contact with the convoy. Five hours later, a likely victim was sighted and preparations were made for a torpedo attack just as the U-boat was sighted by Allied aircraft. Once more *U-85* submerged. Greger surfaced again to follow the convoy through drifting icebergs for the next five hours. The U-boat was again spotted, this time by a destroyer, as she prepared for firing. A single depth charge followed as she submerged but there was no damage.

An hour later, *U-85* resumed pursuit on the surface. The U-boat skirted the convoy, using her faster speed, and took up a waiting position ahead. She submerged before the approaching convoy and at last, had her chance. Two torpedoes were fired at a 7,000-ton merchant ship — and both missed. Single torpedoes were later released at two freighters but observation of the results was interrupted by escort vessels bearing down on the U-boat. She submerged while her torpedoes were still on track but a single detonation, heard as the water closed over her, told the crew that *U-85* had scored. She had, indeed. According to the Naval Historical Branch, Ministry of Defense, London, England, the British SS *Thistleglen,* 4,748 tons, had been hit and went to the bottom.

U-85, meanwhile, had her own problems with the escort vessels. She dropped to a depth of 306 feet and then shuddered from the impact of repeated depth charge detonations. She survived, but for over three hours, each attempt to surface was met by attacking aircraft. For three more hours, *U-85* remained submerged. Then she re-surfaced under "All Clear" conditions to repair her damage and set course for home, St. Nazaire on the Nazi-occupied French Atlantic coast. She had been out for 15 days, the last one-and-a-half playing tag with the convoy, but she had a ship to her credit. She had also contributed to a great German victory by finding the convoy. The battle had cost Germany two U-boats, *U-207* and *U-501,* but 65,409 tons of Allied shipping had been destroyed.

St. Nazaire provided welcome relief for the

U-boat pens at St. Nazaire, France, originally covered by a roof of reinforced concrete, 16 feet thick. When Britain introduced the "Blockbuster" bomb, the Germans countered by increasing the thickness to almost 25 feet. The Allied Air Forces flew so many missions against St. Nazaire and other Bay of Biscay ports that the area surrounding the U-boat pens was totally flattened. Despite saturation bombing, very few U-boats were lost in these ports. The U-boat pens remained operational until the U-boats left because of the approach of Allied land forces. Courtesy of National Archives.

crew. Their mission had been short because of the intensity of the action, but the hours of agonized concern that neither they nor their boat would survive must have seemed endless.

SECOND MISSION

By October 16, repairs and reprovisioning completed, with torpedoes replenished, *U-85* left port on her second war voyage. Five days out, German air surveillance reported an Allied convoy. *U-85* set off in hot pursuit, only to abandon the chase a day later because of rain squalls, heavy seas, bad visibility, and a long-range bomber that the U-boat eluded by submerging, but too late to avoid being sighted. Three depth charges followed her down. They were followed by another three, but no damage was done — except to discourage thought of further pursuit of that convoy.

Four days later, *U-85* joined a pack of U-boats assigned off the coast of Newfoundland. The wolf-pack pounced on a sighted convoy. Before the Allied vessels could disperse into fog, one of the U-boats, not *U-85,* sank three of them. In another instance, fog and heavy seas discouraged

all thought of pursuing another convoy that was reported on *U-85*'s 19th day at sea. As a final touch to compound the problems of a thus far unsuccessful mission, the U-boat's starboard engine broke down. The major problem required 22 hours to replace valves, bearing bolts, and force pumps. Then, low on fuel and lower in spirits, *U-85* headed back to her base in France with a full supply of torpedoes still intact.

Shore leave re-kindled the spirits of the crew during the overhaul of their U-boat at St. Nazaire. While they were enjoying their respite on December 7, 1941, Germany's ally Japan involved them in an expansion of the war that was to cost their lives. That day, Japan attacked the massive American base at Pearl Harbor and the United States responded the following day with a declaration of war against Japan. Germany countered, three days later, by declaring war against the United States.

THIRD WAR CRUISE

The overhauled and reprovisioned *U-85* left port with several other U-boats on January 10, 1942, for her third war assignment — this time to the Mediterranean. Shipboard monotony, for a full week, was disturbed only by a few aircraft alarms, a destroyer alarm, and minor engine repair. Before reaching Gibraltar, *U-85* received orders to proceed to the American coast for agressive action against the new foe. The day after the U-boat changed course, a lone Allied merchant ship came into view, but not for long. *U-85* started in pursuit but was soon out-distanced by the faster freighter. Fast merchant ships frequently went on their own rather than in slow convoy. A convoy's speed was determined by its slowest ship.

Three days later, another sighting was equally unproductive. Then, sighting a vessel zig-zagging at 10 knots on a mean north-easterly course in poor visibility, Captain Greger fired four torpedoes. Without waiting for results, he submerged to 65 feet and waited. Almost six minutes after the torpedoes had been fired, two explosions signalled a dual hit. When his hydrophone reflected only silence from the target area, Greger brought his boat up to periscope depth for observation. The ship was still afloat but, by his report, listing heavily to port. He decided not to use any more of his torpedoes on a ship that would almost surely go down from the damage she had already sustained. When he resurfaced about 30 minutes later the sea was clear. That led Greger to conclude that the vessel had gone down. But she had not.

The Naval Historical Branch, Ministry of Defense, London, has established that the target ship was almost certainly the homeward bound *Port Wyndham,* a British freighter of 8,580 tons. At the time, she would have been in about the position of the attack, and her speed and course matched Greger's description. She also fit the single-funnel, two-masted, 9,000 tons characteristics reported by Greger. Questioned later, the *Port Wyndham* crew were completely unaware of the attack. Records reflect no ship lost at the time in that vicinity. What happened? It is most probable that all torpedoes missed the target, and the two explosions heard by hydrophone were either from another source or detonation of two torpedoes at the end of their long, six minute run. A fast, zig-zagging target in a rough sea is not easy to hit. The U-boat's log reflects that the firing data was imprecise and there were no visual observations to confirm a hit. The heavy list observed by Greger would not be unusual in the prevailing moderate to rough sea. Nor is it a surprise that the crew of *Port Wyndham* were unaware of exploding torpedoes. They would have detonated distant from the freighter and underwater.

Jubilant in their belief that they had sunk the large British ship, Greger and his crew resumed course for the American coast. An enemy steamer, sighted the following day, brought the U-boat into immediate but futile pursuit. The faster merchant ship easily outran *U-85*. Two days passed. Then, a "shooting gallery" prize came into view, a merchant ship at rest, dead in the water. Captain Greger carefully considered the situation. Decoys had been used against U-boats by the British during World War I. Harmless looking merchant vessels were converted into disguised warships for use against U-boats. The Q ships, as they were called, were compartmentalized to avoid sinking if they were hit by one or two torpedoes. A battery of powerful deck guns, concealed behind a false front, could be uncovered in seconds. Such vessels were not used frequently in World War II, but U-boat captains were constantly on the alert to avoid such a trap. Perhaps this placid victim, sighted by Greger, was being offered as bait to tempt him into an imprudent attack. He decided not to take the risk and withdrew.

Four uneventful days later, off the coast of Newfoundland, the U-boat was forced to submerge by an aircraft attack. The one bomb that was dropped was a "near miss" that caused concern but no damage. For another nine days, the U-boat remained off Newfoundland with only two air alarms and a sighting that escaped in a rain squall. After 28 days at sea, *U-85* headed for New York. Two days later, she took off after a merchant ship and pursued it for another day before getting into firing position for a submerged attack. Alerted by the U-boat's periscope, the intended victim zig-zagged out of range, with *U-85* surfaced in fast pursuit. After eight hours, in position 44°45' N, 47°25' W, the U-boat fired a spread of four torpedoes. Only one hit, but that was enough. The Naval Historical Branch, Ministry of Defense, London, has identified the victim as the British SS *Empire Fusilier,* 5,408 tons. She sank within one minute. Greger surfaced to confirm the sinking, then, low on fuel, set course for France. He had left St. Nazaire after an unproductive mission. Forty-six days later, he would return with two sinkings to his credit. One was real, the other a phantom.

FINAL MISSION

Repairs, reprovisioning, and restocking torpedoes readied *U-85* for her fourth war cruise while her crew enjoyed one month ashore — their last shore leave. The U-boat once more headed for American waters on March 21, 1942. Six days after *U-85* left St. Nazaire, that port was heavily damaged by British commandos. That brief span may have meant the difference between death and survival for the U-boat and her crew. Had *U-85* still been in port, the damage inflicted by the attack might have aborted her last mission.

Nineteen days out of St. Nazaire, *U-85* reached the United States coast. Two days later, April 10, an Allied merchant ship, the Norwegian freighter *Chr. Knudsen,* was attacked with two torpedoes. Both hit, and the 4,904-ton vessel quickly sank. Then three days passed with no further action. By then, the U-boat had reached the entrance to Chesapeake Bay. Just past midnight, April 14, *U-85* prowled the surface off the entrance to the bay on a calm sea and under clear skies. Visual observation was perfect. Nothing on the sea could remain undetected, but not a merchant vessel was in sight.

At that moment, the American destroyer, *Roper* (DD147), was on patrol only one-and-a-half miles distant, 14 miles off Nags Head, North Carolina. Action Stations sounded as the warship leaped into pursuit, her radar locked in contact with the unsuspecting U-boat. The range decreased to one mile and *Roper*'s sonar picked up the propellers of the submarine. By then, Greger knew of the destroyer's presence — and his own exposure. The U-boat had been caught in shallow water, only 90 feet deep. To submerge would be suicide and to flee would be futile; the destroyer would quickly overtake the U-boat on the surface. Only one option lay open — fight, hope, and pray.

Roper closed to less than half a mile as Greger fired a torpedo in desperation. The approaching warship's slender bow presented too small a target, but there was all to gain and nothing to lose. The long torpedo streaked from the U-boat's single, stern tube. Time suspended as the sleek gray cylinder headed for the prow of the onrushing enemy vessel. The torpedo passed the bow of the destroyer and narrowly missed her port beam. Then, time restarted.

Roper was rapidly overtaking as *U-85* veered sharply to starboard. The destroyer's 24" searchlight flooded the U-boat and made positive identification. The U-boat continued her hard turn to starboard. With shorter turning radius, Greger hoped to bring the forward torpedo tubes to bear on the destroyer. The maneuver failed, but it did open the distance between the two vessels — some, but not enough. The U-boat, bathed in the glare of the searchlight, made an easy target for the American destroyer's 3" battery and 50 caliber guns. Greger's men tried to man their 88mm deck gun, but the machine guns of the destroyer drove them to a precarious shelter behind the conning tower. The end came quickly as a 3" gun manned by a young coxswain, Harry Heyman, who had never before shot in combat, shattered the conning tower. *U-85* began to sink, stern first, as the German crew scrambled out in the glare of *Roper*'s searchlight. The destroyer's crew looked on in disbelief as the U-boat went under rapidly.

USS *Roper (DD-147),* under command of Lt. Commander Hamilton Wilcox Howe. The destroyer caught *U-85* surfaced in shallow water. Courtesy of National Archives.

Three months after onset of "Operation Paukenschlag," the U-boat offensive that was staged off United States shores, *Roper* scored America's first success against the German raiders. The illustration shows *U-85,* straddled by gunfire, silhouetted in the glare of a searchlight. Painting by Alfred "Chief" Johnson, courtesy of the Singer Company, Librascope Division.

They reasoned that the damaged conning tower could not have been the reason. Only intentional scuttling would have taken her down so fast.

Roper's Captain, Lieutenant Commander Hamilton Wilcox Howe, ordered depth charges dropped. He wanted to ensure that the U-boat was indeed destroyed. The destroyer steamed through the waters cluttered with shouting German sailors to drop 11 depth charges over the U-boat. No effort was made to rescue the survivors from the water for fear that another U-boat might be lurking in the area to take advantage of such a diversion. Finally, after daylight a search for survivors and debris was conducted by a PBY (U.S. patrol/reconnaissance flying boat) aircraft commanded by Lieutenant C.V. Horrigan, USNR. Oil slicks and floating corpses were all that marked the location. Three more depth charges were then dropped, one by the PBY, the other two by *Roper,* to ensure that the U-boat was really destroyed. For his action as commander of *Roper,* Lieutenant Commander Howe received the Navy Cross for destruction of Germany's

"Wild Boar."

Twenty-nine bodies were recovered during the morning search. Two more, both badly mauled by depth charges or *Roper*'s churning propellers, were allowed to sink after a thorough search of their clothing for items of possible interest to U.S. Naval Intelligence. Two of the recovered bodies had tubing from escape lung mouthpieces in their mouths, evidence that they may have escaped after the U-boat went to the bottom.

Much of the *U-85* story is based on the contents of small diaries carried by two of the German seamen, Stabsobermaschinist (Chief Machinist) Eugen Ungethum and another, Erich Degenkolb. They ignored the orders of Admiral Dönitz and not only carried, but kept current, personal diaries of events aboard *U-85.* Very little else of value to Naval Intelligence was recovered from the victims or the water. Before leaving the site, *Roper* set an orange buoy over the U-boat's wreckage. Then, the twenty-nine recovered bodies were transferred to USS *Scioto* for transfer to the Norfolk Naval Base.

U-85 casualties being transferred from *Roper* to *Scioto*. Courtesy of National Archives.

The gruesome task of transferring *U-85* casualties continues. Courtesy of National Archives.

U-85 casualties heaped on stern of *Scioto*. Courtesy of National Archives.

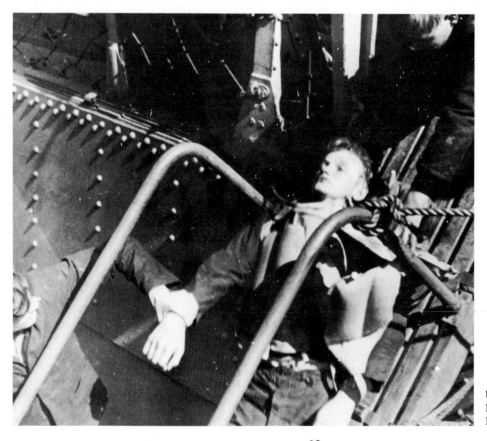

Unloading *U-85* casualties at Norfolk Naval Base. Courtesy of National Archives.

Corpses of *U-85* crewmen laid out in small hangar at Norfolk Air Station. Courtesy of National Archives.

Fifty-two prisoners, all from Fort Monroe, Virginia, prepared graves for *U-85* casualties. Courtesy of National Archives.

The caskets, in boxes, containing corpses of *U-85* crewmen were unloaded from trucks to be placed in individual graves. Courtesy of National Archives.

The corpses of the German sailors were laid out in a small hangar at the Norfolk Air Station. They were photographed and identified through I.D. tags, clothing tabs, or other personal effects. Captain Greger's body was not among those recovered. Burial services at the Hampton National Cemetery, Virginia, were conducted on April 15. They included participation by Catholic and Protestant clergy and full military honors, including 20 Military Police pall-bearers. A three volley gun salute by 24 U.S. Navy seamen and the mournful strains of "Taps" marked the passing of at least 29 of the *U-85* crew.

At 8 P.M., April 15, 1942, the burial service for *U-85* casualties was read by the Catholic Chaplain, followed by the Protestant Chaplain. The firing party of U.S. seamen fired three volleys, and "Taps" was sounded. The Germans had died at night and were buried at night. Courtesy of U.S. Naval Institute.

The graves of *U-85* crewmen at the Hampton National Cemetery, Virginia, share the final resting place of American casualties — on American soil. Courtesy of National Archives.

SALVAGE EFFORT

On the day of the burial, a British Navy trawler, *Bedfordshire*, left Norfolk, commissioned to locate the U-boat for U.S Naval Intelligence. The trawler snagged *U-85* with a grapnell after a two day search. The position was logged at 35°55' N, 75°15' W, 14 miles off Nags Head, N.C. When a diver descended to explore the wreck, he found the visibility so poor, that the effort was abandoned until conditions improved. *Bedfordshire* was then ordered off for convoy duty, her place taken by USS *Keywadin*. A few days later, with improved visibility, diving resumed and an unexploded depth charge was discovered close to the hull of the U-boat. Diving was suspended until the depth charge hazard was eliminated by a Mine Disposal Unit from the Washington Navy Yard.

The salvage vessel USS *Falcon* was enlisted to raise the wreck from its shallow, 90 foot depth. From April 30 till May 5, 1942, the Navy made 78 dives to the U-boat. One diver penetrated the open conning tower hatch, a major accomplishment considering the cumbersome, surface-tended, hard hat diving outfit he was wearing in such close quarters. Inside, he found the hatch to the control room slightly ajar. Tempted though he was, he decided that his bulky gear made it too

dangerous to go further. He retreated, closing the conning tower hatch behind him to keep the compartment water-tight for the planned salvage.

Divers recovered the 20mm anti-aircraft gun for Naval Intelligence study. Other items included the 88mm deck gun sight, the night firing device, the gyro pelorus repeater, and the gyro steering repeater from the bridge. Naval Intelligence would also have liked to obtain a torpedo stowed under the deck, but it could not be freed for removal.

One diver discovered that the forward torpedo tubes were loaded and the doors were open, ready to be fired. Had Greger succeeded in gaining firing position with his tight turn to starboard, the destroyer might have been disabled or sunk and the U-boat might then have escaped into deeper waters.

Lieutenant G.K. Mackensie, commanding the operation, reported that *U-85* had been thoroughly and efficiently scuttled by her crew. All internal compartments had been flooded and the external salvage air lines had collapsed. Only extensive pontooning could raise her. The Navy considered such an operation too dangerous for the duration of the war because of the constant threat of U-boats in the area. *U-85* was left at rest — until sport divers arrived on the scene 33 years later.

USS *Falcon (ASR-2)*, a tender and salvage ship for submarines, conducted many salvage operations *(S-5, S-51, Squalus,* and *0-9)* after her commissioning in November 1918. By 1942, when she attempted the salvage of *U-85*, she was aging but still able. However, the U-boat had been efficiently scuttled by her crew and the threat of U-boats in the area prohibited the salvage attempt. Courtesy of U.S. Naval Historical Center.

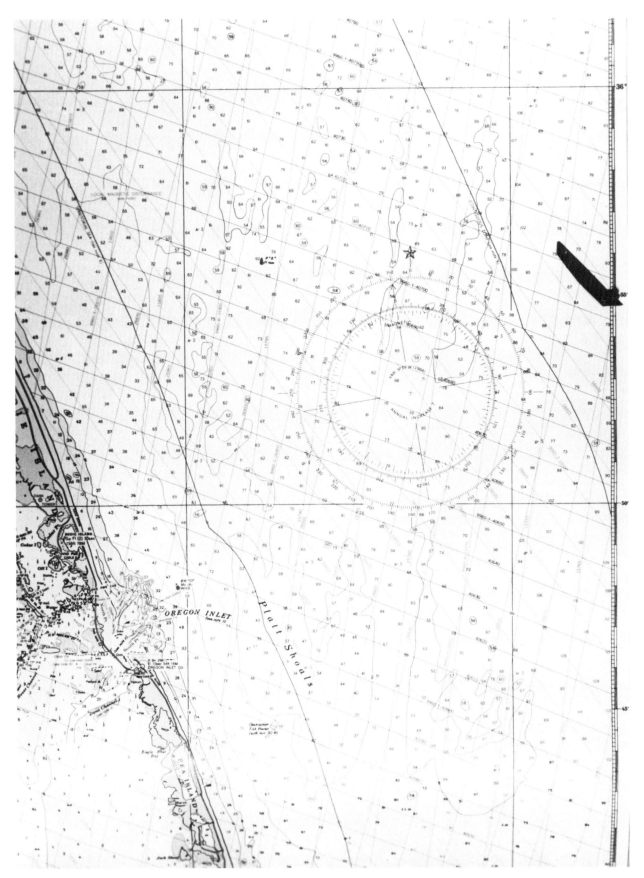

U-85 was sunk at 35° 55′ N, 75° 15′ W, 17 miles northeast of Oregon Inlet, North Carolina. This illustration should not be used for navigational purposes.

SPORT DIVING

By 1975, diving had developed into an exciting sport for thousands of daring amateurs. Self-contained diving equipment, advanced scuba diving techniques, and the development of organized groups of divers sharing a common interest combined to focus attention on shipwrecks, at depths shallow enough for scuba diving.

One major group of divers of the period was the Eastern Divers Association, established in the mid 60's by avid wreck enthusiasts from several states. Its membership was high in enthusiasm but low in organization until 1969, when a charismatic, demanding leader, Tom Roach, took over as President and headed the group for the next nine years. Roach first learned about *U-85* from a New Jersey dive boat captain, Skip Gallamore, who chartered a dive to the U-boat in 1975. Roach weaned the loran numbers from someone and chartered another New Jersey dive boat captain, George Hoffman, to take members of his association to the wreck. They were rewarded with the opportunity to view the historic remains and the artifacts that abounded on the U-boat's deck and in the surrounding sand. Shells from the 88mm deck gun that might have saved *U-85* had they been used, were still in their water-tight containers. Several open hatches invited easy access to the interior where dinnerware such as German Navy plates and cups were recovered as memoribelia and additions to display collections.

Other charters provided rewarding and unexpected finds such as Larry Keen experienced. Keen, a diver for 25 years, was groping through the silt in the control room, blinded by the sediment-filled water. He was happy because he had already recovered the U-boat's compass. Then his fingers found the sharp sides of a small box. With no chance to examine it in the zero visibility, he stuffed the box into his mesh "Bug" bag. Continuing, he grasped a long cylinder that came away easily. Then he withdrew with his collection of artifacts. Aboard the dive boat, Keen examined the cylinder that turned out to be a chart case. It contained charts of the United States coast, but they were badly waterlogged and decomposed. The smell of decay prompted the captain to have them thrown overboard, unaware of their potential value. Within the small wooden box was a fine stop watch that had been used for timing torpedo runs. Spanish doubloons and silver plate provide incentive to many who risk their lives for such treasure, but to a diver like Larry Keen, his historical artifacts have far more significance than treasure. Later, he would be the first to penetrate the control room of another U-boat, *U-352,* wrecked off the eastern seaboard.

Her ease of accessibility, only 17 miles northeast of Oregon Inlet, and depth of only 90 feet combine to make the wreck of *U-85* a popular dive for scuba enthusiasts who come to view the historic remains and gather what artifacts they may be lucky enough to find.

Tom Roach displays *U-85* 88mm shell. Photo by Michael A. deCamp.

A typical U-boat 88mm deck gun, above. The gun developed by the German Navy was in no way related to the Army's 88mm Flak gun. The ammunition was not even interchangeable. Photo below, the same type of gun as it appears today on the deck of *U-85*'s remains. Photo by H. Keatts.

Stopwatch for timing torpedo runs. Found by Larry Keen. Photo by H. Keatts.

Drinking mug — an artifact recovered by Larry Keen. Photo by H. Keatts.

Dinner plate recovered by Larry Keen. Photo by H. Keatts.

U.S. Navy records reflect that the U-boat is lying on her starboard side with a list of 80°. Personal observation confirms the list is indeed severe. The photograph of *U-85*'s deck gun was taken starboard of the U-boat while standing on the bottom facing the exposed deck area.

The wild boar insignia of *U-85* has disappeared. It had been painted on the flak shield protecting the conning tower. Now, the shield has decomposed and the insignia is gone, doomed to extinction on April 14, 1942. But if Captain Greger's maneuvers to turn tables on USS *Roper* had succceded, *U-85* and her "Wild Boar with Rose in Mouth" would have survived to carry on the objectives of Hitler's naval strategists.

Compass recovered by Larry Keen. Photo by H. Keatts.

U.S. Navy divers attempted to remove this reserve torpedo, clamped under *U-85's* deck. Photo by H. Keatts.

CHAPTER SIX

STRATEGIC ERROR — U-352

The fate of ships often can be likened to essential human contradictions: that some ships, like some men may achieve or fail, gain fame or dishonor depending on time, circumstance and luck.

U-352 appeared destined for obscurity. She had never sunk a ship; she was, essentially, a failure. Even her sinking was ignominious. Probably, like "some mute inglorious Milton" of Thomas Gray's "Elegy Written in a Country Churchyard," she should have remained quietly in her grave. She didn't.

War had been in progress since 1939, and U-boat production had been accelerated to win victory for Nazi Germany in the "Battle of the Atlantic." The years 1940 and '41 were the "Happy Time" of Germany's U-boat campaign. Allied merchant ships were being sunk, almost at will, by bold underwater or even surface U-boat attacks. Underwater life was a cramped, damp, and sickening existence. The combined smells of unwashed bodies, fuel, and food penetrated every crevice with a stench to challenge even the strongest stomachs. It was a lonely existence, with everything tasting of diesel oil and flavored with mold. Still, U-boat recruitment flourished. Public relations experts spared no expense to promote the exploits of U-boats such as the glorified *U-37,* which in May, 1940, had sunk 11 enemy ships for a total of over 43,000 tons. And five months later *U-99* was credited with the war's record for a single U-boat patrol: seven ships totaling 65,137 tons. Her commander, Otto Kretchmer, then went on to become one of the highest scoring U-boat commanders of World War II, with 44 ships totaling 266,629 tons to his credit.

Dreams of glory made every moment out of combat a lost opportunity for the crew of *U-352,* but five months would pass before the new U-boat was commissioned. She was one of 1,150 U-boats launched in Germany's bid for domination of Allied shipping lanes — an objective that almost became a reality.

The "Battle of the Atlantic," was to cost Germany two thirds of her 1,150 U-boats and 33,000 of the 40,000 sailors who manned them. Blissfully unaware that they would be contributing to those loss statistics, the crew of *U-352* pulsed with impatience as their boat was being outfitted for her war duties.

THE U-BOAT

U-352 was a Type VIIC U-boat. The new type, introduced in 1940, increased size and displacement over VIIB to accommodate more fuel and torpedoes. She measured 220 feet with a 20' 3" beam, displaced 769 tons, and was equipped with additional communications equipment over the earlier Type VIIB. *U-352* carried a complement of 46, with Kapitänleutnant Hellmut Rathke in command. The 31-year-old ardent Nazi had served for six years on surface vessels before his U-boat command. Rathke was inexperienced underwater, but he was an effective disciplinarian. He quickly molded the crew to his thinking, a process that gained him the dedicated respect of each man and a high level of discipline that was later to frustrate the determined efforts of the United States military to extract information from his men.

Finally commissioned in mid-October, *U-352* left Flensburg for Kiel, on the Baltic coast, to undergo four weeks of check-out tests. Her

Kapitänleutnant Hellmut Rathke, commander of *U-352*. Courtesy of Ed Caram.

conning tower proudly displayed the Flensburg coat-of-arms, symbol that the city had adopted the U-boat as its own. One day, Flensburg might share in the glory of *U-352,* with the Führer himself bestowing the coveted Knight's Cross on her commander under the Flensburg emblem.

FIRST WAR CRUISE

Late in November, after final trials and tactical exercises, the U-boat returned to Flensburg for minor repairs and adjustments. Finally headed for action, she left for Kiel in mid-January, 1942,

Like a number of other U-boats, *U-352* was adopted by a German city. She proudly displayed the Flensburg coat-of-arms on her conning tower. Courtesy of Goethe House, New York, Cultural Center.

U-352 commissioning ceremony. Courtesy of Ed Caram.

A *U-352* crewman raises the Kriegsmarine ensign for the first time. Courtesy of Ed Caram.

to stock provisions and torpedoes. Then, armed with an 88mm cannon and a 20mm anti-aircraft gun, *U-352* set out on her first war cruise. Anticipation ran high as the new U-boat stopped overnight at Bergen, Norway, then headed for her operational assignment: to interrupt Allied shipping south of Iceland. For three weeks, the exciting prospect of a sinking gave way to the abrasive monotony of cramped existence, interrupted only by frequent enemy air attacks. It was a far cry from the heroic visions of glory that had earlier supported the crew's spirit. Is this, they wondered, what war is all about? Would the mission be wasted without even an enemy sighting?

Jubilation swept the U-boat as a convoy came into view. Excitement and speculation ran high as action stations were ordered, torpedo doors opened, and torpedoes readied. Then, over the horizon, four enemy escort vessels appeared. Rathke quickly aborted the attack and submerged, but not before the U-boat had been sighted. The depth charges that followed provided some very respectable explosions but no damage of consequence according to one of the crew.

Two weeks later, without sighting another enemy vessel, Rathke set course for St. Nazaire, the U-boat's home base in France. A full load of torpedoes was still aboard but five weeks of unproductive patrol had left *U-352* as low in fuel as in spirit. En route, Rathke sighted a distant enemy destroyer. He knew the likelihood of a hit at that distance was remote, but so too was the risk of counter-attack. He fired a fan of four torpedoes, but the destroyer evidenced no awareness of the action. The firing may have been intended to relieve the crew's frustration. For whatever reason, *U-352* could now return from her fruitless mission, with a claim of action against an enemy warship and four torpedoes expended.

Forty-four days after her departure from Kiel, the U-boat reached St. Nazaire, ending her first war cruise in disappointment and dejection. In an unwarranted formal reception, three members of the crew were awarded Iron Crosses — a good psychological note by the public relations-minded German High Command.

After spending a day cleaning the vessel, the crew transferred to quarters ashore. Most were granted leave; two even returned to Germany to be married. Only one crew member remained aboard to monitor the engine overhaul that would take one month. Three weeks later, a British commando raid seriously damaged St. Nazaire repair facilities and lock gates. But *U-352*

escaped unscathed and her crew, quartered away from the harbor, were unharmed.

SECOND AND LAST WAR CRUISE

Nine days after the raid *U-352* headed through the only undamaged lock for her second war cruise. It was April 5, only six months since she had been commissioned, but the U-boat would never return. *U-352* and her crew might have shared a far different fate if the one undamaged lock had been destroyed by the British.

Clear of St. Nazaire, the U-boat headed directly for Cape Hatteras and American waters, an area that was already called the "Graveyard of the Atlantic." Rathke hoped to add his share of enemy ships to the many already littering the bottom. The crossing was slow in order to conserve fuel. It took *U-352* almost a month to reach the coast of the United States. It was May 2, and sightings were made almost immediately. Several unsuccessful attempts were made against merchant ships while a constant air attack alert was maintained against the U-boat's most serious threat — air attack. On May 7, the U-boat was sighted by an aircraft that dropped two bombs. Although the pilot claimed a "kill," *U-352* escaped undamaged. That night Rathke received a long-awaited message. German Intelligence reported a convoy that would pass through his operational area in the next few days.

FATAL MISTAKE

Tension mounted. The moment for *U-352* to prove her worth was at hand. Now she would surely earn her niche in the archives of Germany. The citizens of Flensburg soon would have ample reason to be proud of their adopted U-boat. Tempo quickened aboard the U-boat on May 9, 1942, as a silhouette took shape on the horizon — one of the convoy vessels! Rathke ordered "Action Stations" to a crew that almost anticipated his command. He maneuvered *U-352* into position, carefully sighted, and fired a single torpedo. Then, he gasped in dismay. It was not the small merchant ship he had supposed her to be, but a small American warship. He was in shallow waters, where the odds of escape from a depth charge attack were against him. His only hope was that the running torpedo would hold course and strike a crippling blow.

Rathke's hopes were dashed. The torpedo exploded prematurely, 200 yards short of the port quarter of the American target. She was *Icarus,* a Coast Guard cutter en route from Staten Island, New York to Key West, Florida. Even before the explosion, sonar had alerted *Icarus'* Captain, Lieutenant Commander Maurice D. Jester, U.S.C.G., to the U-boat's presence. Rathke

TYPE VIIC

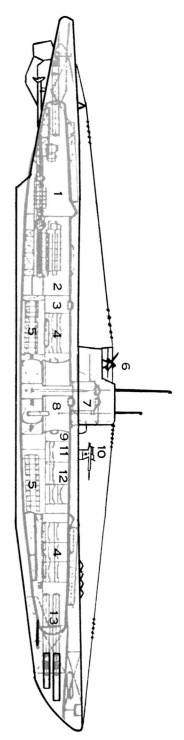

1. Aft torpedo room & electric motor
2. Diesel engine room
3. Galley
4. Crew quarters
5. Batteries
6. 20mm anti-aircraft gun
7. Conning tower

8. Control room
9. Radio room
10. 88mm deck gun
11. Commander's quarters
12. Officer's quarters
13. Forward torpedo room

Displacement (tons)
  Surfaced 769
  Submerged 871
Length .... 220'3"
Beam .... 20'3"
Draught .... 15'9"
Fuel capacity (tons) 114
Speed (knots)
  Surfaced 17.75
  Submerged 7.5
Range (nautical miles/kn.)
  Surfaced 8,850/10
  Submerged 80/4
Armament
  Bow torpedo tubes 4
  Stern torpedo tubes 1
  Torpedoes carried (number/size) .... 14/21"
  Guns (number/size) .... 1/20mm — 1/88mm
Crew 44

Icarus, a 165-foot United States Coast Guard cutter, sank the 220-foot *U-352.* Courtesy of National Archives.

headed into the churning waters of the explosion area, hoping to throw off pursuit. Jester anticipated the maneuver and took position directly over the turbulence. He ordered a diamond pattern of five depth charges to a depth of 100 feet, then three additional charges in a "V" pattern. Another charge was dropped over the site when large bubbles boiled to the surface.

The first pass destroyed *U-352*'s attack periscope and killed her Executive Officer. The hull of the U-boat shuddered under the barrage of the continuing assault. Shards of glass, crockery, and loose gear flew at random. Crewmen hurtled into obstacles and one another with crippling violence. The electrical system was destroyed, leaving no electric propulsion and only emergency lighting. In the dim carnage, the U-boat lay stripped of means for escape or battle.

The second attack had broached the pressure hull in the forward torpedo room, drowning part of the crew. The damaging single charge that followed discouraged all hope of escape. Rathke ordered the battered crew to don escape lungs and life jackets and ballast tanks blown. The U-boat shot to the surface, 44 minutes after initial sonar contact by *Icarus.* "Abandon Ship" was ordered and the well-disciplined crew passed through the conning tower with clock-work precision — into a hail of gunfire.

Icarus had opened fire as the U-boat hit the surface. Her 50 caliber and 30 caliber machine guns raked the deck. Then, the 3 inch deck gun moved into action at 800 yards. The first two shots straddled the hull but the third was a direct hit on the conning tower. Six of the next 11 rounds struck the battered conning tower or hull. Germans and Americans later agreed that if *U-352*'s deck guns had been brought into action, they might have sunk *Icarus* and the U-boat might have limped off to safety. Only the immediate action and accuracy of the cutter's gun crews kept the German 88mm deck gun and 20mm anti-aircraft gun neutralized.

Only five minutes after blowing to the surface, *U-352* plunged back down with two officers and 11 crewmen. There she remains at latitude 34°12' N, longitude 76°35' W. The site is 26 miles south of Beaufort Inlet, North Carolina in 115 feet of water. Before abandoning the U-boat, Rathke had ordered scuttling charges set. Their muffled explosions were heard on the surface as the German crew struggled in the ocean. Ignoring the survivors, Jester ordered another depth charge dropped on the sunken U-boat to assure that she remained out of action. Then, he radioed for instructions regarding the Germans. He received orders from the 6th Naval District to bring them to Charleston. As *Icarus* moved in to pick up survivors, security-conscious Rathke warned his men not to divulge information to their rescuers. Then, he asked the cutter's crew to take his wounded aboard first.

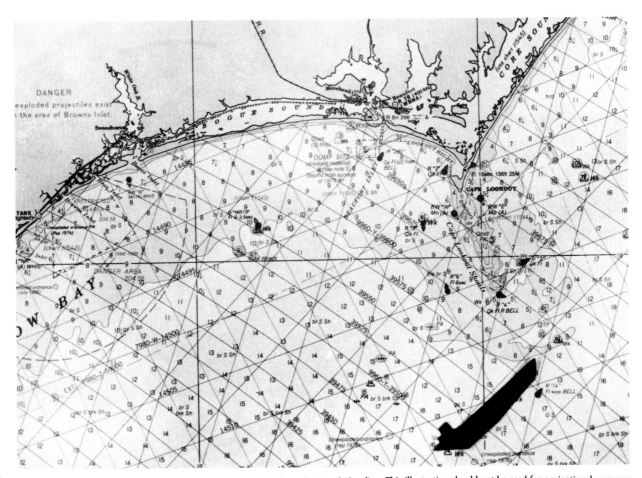

U-352 was sunk at 34° 12′ N, 76° 35′ W, 26 miles south of Beaufort Inlet, North Carolina. This illustration should not be used for navigational purposes.

SURVIVORS

Four survivors, wounded by gunfire, were treated aboard *Icarus*. Rathke, while still in the water, applied a tourniquet to machinist's mate Gerd Reussel, whose leg had been severed. Another crewman lost an arm. All suffered severe headaches from the rapid ascent of the U-boat. With all that, and though they had been in the water for 45 minutes, the prisoners were in good spirits with excellent morale and military manner. A search produced German, French, and Norwegian currency, but only one set of papers that included any form of technical information.

Thirty prisoners were placed under guard in the forward crew compartment. The sailor who had lost an arm and another, seriously injured, were placed under guard in the crew's head. Reussel, who had lost a leg, was placed on a litter to remain on deck for minimum movement and warm, fresh air. His rescuers administered adrenalin and a sedative, but despite those measures, Reussel died at 10:15 P.M. Jester was instructed by the 6th Naval District to bury the German at sea unless the senior of the prisoners objected. Rathke refused approval and the corpse was delivered to Charleston with the survivors. Reussel was buried with military honors in Post Section, grave no. 18, National Cemetery, Beaufort, South Carolina.

Aboard *Icarus,* Rathke reinforced his warning not to divulge information to the Americans. He called on his crew to remember their dead comrades. Jester then isolated Rathke, but the damage had already been done. When questioned by *Icarus* officers, the uncommunicative Germans first claimed they could not speak English. Later, the same prisoners were observed reading English copies of the *Saturday Evening Post*. Three German-speaking *Icarus* crew members were assigned to talk with the prisoners. When asked any question relating to their U-boat, the Germans claimed to not understand; in turn, they asked about the cutter. They would speak freely on personal matters, but had nothing to say on military subjects.

Icarus reached Charleston at 11:30 A.M., the day after her encounter with *U-352*. As Rathke and the U-boat crew left the Coast Guard cutter, the German captain thanked his captor for the treatment provided his men. The District Intelligence Officer at Charleston was as unsuccessful

U.S. Marines stand guard as the 32 survivors of *U-352* line up before *Icarus.* Courtesy of National Archives.

U-352 prisoners display rigid discipline and perfect step as they follow their captain to quarters under U.S. Marine escort. Courtesy of National Archives.

U-352 prisoners Kapitänleutnant Hellmut Rathke, second from left, and Leutnant zur See Oskar Bernard, center, converse with Lt. Commander Frank P. North, USNR, British Lt. Commander Stone, and Commander Sidney W. Souers, USNR, at Charleston Navy Yard barracks. Courtesy of National Archives.

Survivors of *U-352*, at the Charleston Navy Yard, fall to for their first chicken dinner in weeks — the first of many meals during their long imprisonment. Courtesy of National Archives.

Bernard repeats in German the instructions given him by U.S. Navy officers as the crew prepare to eat. Food was served to prisoners in the barracks adjoining the Navy Yard's brig, which may be seen in the background. The German seaman in the foreground, Heinrich Twirdy, had been wounded by machine gun fire as he escaped from the U-boat. Courtesy of National Archives.

interrogating *U-352*'s officers and men as the *Icarus* officers had been. The prisoners were turned over to the Provost Marshall at Paris Island, South Carolina, for transfer to a Detention Camp at Fort Bragg, North Carolina. Throughout, Rathke was permitted to maintain direct control over his men. Three months passed before a special investigating unit of United States and British officers, specially trained in the interrogation of U-boat survivors, was called in to ferret out any information that might help to reduce the undersea menace. Meanwhile, the prisoners had been subjected to constant security lectures by Rathke. If anything useful was learned, it was that future U-boat survivors should be separated immediately, with officers kept apart from the enlisted men and, if at all possible, with the youngest and least intelligent separated into a third group.

Lieutenant Commander Jester was awarded the Navy Cross for his destruction of *U-352*.

On May 19, 1942, the salvage tug USS *Umpqua*

Lt. Commander Maurice D. Jester, USCG, commander of *Icarus*, reads a statement telling how he sank *U-352*. Courtesy of National Archives.

left New York to conduct salvage operations on *U-352* for Naval Intelligence. The U-boat was caught by grappling hook on May 23, and U.S. Navy diver C.E. Meyer inspected the wreck. He reported a submarine lying on her starboard side at an angle of about 60 degrees, with a large hole in her bow. The hose length of his surface-tended hard hat diving outfit prevented a more thorough examination. The salvage tug returned in August but operations were quickly discontinued when on the third dive, several unexploded depth charges were found. To make matters more hazardous, the bottom current was running at 2.5 knots — too strong for hard hat divers to work against.

SPORT DIVING

After the Navy left, *U-352* lay undisturbed for more than 30 years; her only visitors were schools of fish. Meanwhile, sport divers were developing new skills with self-contained underwater breathing apparatus. They were no longer restricted by the hoses and hard hats of surface-tended diving. Areas once beyond reach became playgrounds for the tank-toting scuba divers off for a weekend of exciting exploration.

U-352 at sea. Courtesy of WZ-Bilddienst, Wilhelmshaven, West Germany.

U-352 as she is today. Courtesy of and copyright by Ed Caram, 1983.

Sport divers who had read of U-boats sunk off the North Carolina coast, searched for *U-352,* using Loran-A (Long Range Aid to Navigation) units that provided site location accuracy within 1,000 feet. Their efforts were fruitless. Then, in 1975, George Purifoy a charter boat captain of Morehead City, N.C. replaced Loren-A with Loran-C, a highly sophisticated system that pinpointed location to within 50 feet. With his electronic marvel, a nautical chart with Loran-C overprint, and a graph recording depth sounder, Purifoy launched his search. In only 30 minutes on his first attempt, Purifoy and two friends, Rod Gross and Dale McClough were rewarded when the boat's recording depth sounder outlined a promising object on the bottom. An exploratory dive confirmed their find. *U-352* had been rediscovered.

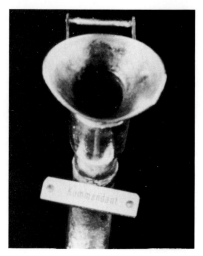

"Kommandant's" voice tube. Photo by Tom Roach.

George Purifoy found *U-352* in 1975. He is shown here with the U-boat's 20mm anti-aircraft gun. Photo by H. Keatts.

Eastern North Carolina quickly developed into a Mecca for scuba divers eager to travel a third of a century back in time into World War II history. *U-352,* in 115 feet of warm, clear Gulfstream waters and only 26 miles offshore, quickly gained a reputation as one of the most popular dive attractions of the east coast. She offered the venturesome a wide range of artifacts.

The U-boat's publicity came to the attention of Larry Keen, a diver for 25 years and member of the Eastern Divers Association, a group of experienced wreck divers. Keen's diving interest stemmed from a Christmas gift of Cousteau's *The Silent World* in 1950. The book stimulated his interest in a new world of adventure, as it has for multitudes of others. The following year, Keen and a friend brought Wilmington, Delaware into the diving community by opening its first dive shop. Two years later he purchased a dive charter boat to launch a serious search for shipwrecks. Then, in 1972, Keen dove the sunken U-boat, *U-853,* off Block Island, R.I. From that day, he has retained his avid interest in sunken submarines. He no longer operates his diver shop, but he does captain a charter boat out of Ocean City, Maryland.

When Keen learned the location of *U-352,* he scheduled several dive trips to the wreck during 1976. He was first to enter the U-boat's control room, the fulfillment of every diver's dream. Others before him had penetrated the interior through an open hatch into the forward torpedo room and worked their way aft toward the control room. There, they were stopped. Across the hatch opening, a heavy steel bar had jammed into position, allowing a limited view of the interior but effectively blocking further passage.

Following the same route used by others before him, Keen reached the forward torpedo room. From there, it was only about 30 feet aft to the control room. On the surface, 30 feet is simple, but in penetrating a shipwreck, it is a challenging and hazardous experience. The problems are magnified when the wreck happens to be a submarine designed for economy of space, not comfort. To make matters worse, visibility is clouded by microscopic organisms and sediment. Even a powerful dive light does little to improve visibility.

More by touch than vision, Keen worked his way through the 30 feet of passageway and hatches to the blocked control room entry. To have come this far and then be denied was beyond his credence. He extended an arm forward through the opening. There was plenty of clearance for at least that part of him. Suddenly, he had the solution. Why, he wondered, hadn't it occurred to others? Careful to disturb the heavy silt as little as possible, he removed his air tanks and pushed them forward through the opening into the room. Then, he squeezed under the bar and there he was, the first to occupy the control room of *U-352* since the flight of her crew from the stricken U-boat 34 years earlier.

In silence, broken only by the intermittent stream of air bubbles from his own regulator, Keen surveyed his prize. Marine life and corrosion had reduced much of the instrumentation to general outlines. But improved access and time would soon see the removal of growth, corrosion, and the cherished artifacts they covered by scores of scuba divers to follow. Then he discovered at

A school of fish swim past an open hatch. Photo by Tom Roach.

U-352's attack periscope, later removed by scuba divers. Photo by Tom Roach.

his feet proof that he indeed was the first to have penetrated into the control room. A sextant and a pair of German binoculars lay there, and no one would have passed up such cherished prizes.

With little time left, he gathered the artifacts, squeezed back under the bar, pulled his air tanks through, donned them, and started his return. Getting back out is even more difficult than entry because as a diver swims forward, sediment stirs up behind, reducing visibility to zero. Under extreme conditions, divers leave their swim fins outside a wreck to avoid disturbing the silt and pull themselves along by hand. Keen, had not deemed it necessary to remove his fins. He exited successfully. Since his initial entry, the steel bar barrier has been cut away by other divers. Control room access no longer requires removal of a diver's air tanks.

In the fall of 1979, 40-year-old Dave Bluett of Vienna, Virginia, 30-year-old Fran Gibel of Silver Spring, Maryland, and 64-year-old Howard

Caulk, also of Silver Spring, recovered the five foot portside propeller from the U-boat. However, the prize had cost them almost a year of frustration.

In late 1978, the three divers, using 30- and 50-ton hydraulic jacks borrowed from the Maryland Ship and Drydock Company, had failed to free the propeller. The following spring, they attempted to force it off with pneumatic chisels, tried to loosen it with muriatic acid, and even applied super-cold liquid dioxide in an attempt to shrink the shaft. The propeller would not budge. On September 29, 1979 one more attempt was made to free the stubborn prop. Bluett, the driving force behind the salvage project, had made six spreaders with three metal turnbuckles to apply 120 tons of pressure. With the spreaders in position, Bluett applied pressure and he

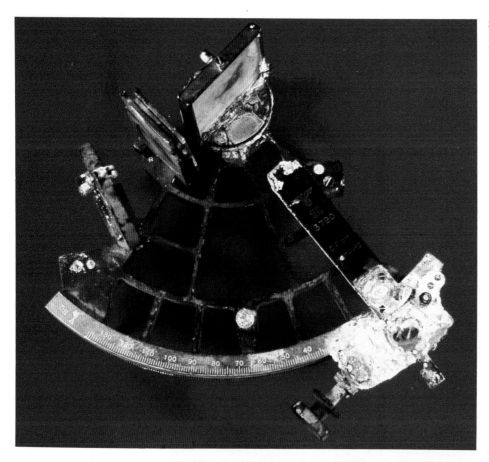

Sextant found by Larry Keen in *U-352*'s control room. Photo by H. Keatts.

Zeiss binoculars, also found by Larry Keen in *U-352*'s control room. Photo by H. Keatts.

blinked in surprise as the balky propeller started to move. A year of frustration had ended. When the prop finally fell from the shaft the trio attached lift bags to the massive artifact and sent it to the surface where it was winched aboard a trawler.

Unfortunately, the U-boat also attracted the attention of a few insensitive divers who took macabre satisfaction from removing and displaying skeletal remains of the U-boat's crew. A United States Senator and the Federal Republic of Germany have classified the U-boat "A National War Grave." The Senator labeled the removal of German skeletal remains a national disgrace, an opinion shared by the vast majority of American sport divers. They feel maligned by association with the vandals because their only bond is a mutual interest in scuba sport diving. Whether by peer pressure, shame, or fear of reprisal, such violations no longer occur on *U-352*. Other such ghoul-like actions by irresponsible scuba divers should precipitate immediate action by government agencies, scuba associations, and individual divers to purge the desecrators from sport diving.

DANGEROUS ORDNANCE

Word spread rapidly of the artifacts being

This propeller was removed by scuba divers since the photograph was taken. Photo by Tom Roach.

Skeletal remains of *U-352's* crew, subject of international controversy. Photo by Tom Roach.

Hundreds of fish school over and around an artificial reef — *U-352*'s conning tower. Photo by H. Keatts.

During the U.S. Navy survey, a torpedo warhead was located topside on *U-352*. Courtesy of U.S. Navy.

recovered and the unexploded ordnance in and about the U-boat. One torpedo protruded from the stern torpedo tube, 20mm and 88mm shells lay scattered about the wreck, and one torpedo rested in the sand with its warhead under the U-boat. Safety devices protected the torpedoes from explosion to ensure that they did not detonate inside the U-boat. A safety lock capping the warhead spun itself off a threaded shaft after the torpedo had run approximately 90 feet through the water. But corrosion, after 34 years underwater, might have destroyed the effectiveness of the safety controls.

Such unexploded torpedoes pose a threat not only to divers but also to net dragging fishermen. On July 19, 1965, the trawler *Snoopy*, became the last vessel to be sunk by a World War II German torpedo — one that had become entangled in her net. In another such incident, a trawler from Norfolk, Virginia caught a German torpedo. The vessel remained afloat after the resulting explosion killed several of her crew.

Word of the hazard came to the attention of United States Senator Lowell Weicker (R-Conn.), a certified scuba diver. He visited the wreck on July 16, 1978. His dive confirmed all he had been told. *U-352* did indeed pose a serious, potential threat. The following day, he addressed a request to the Secretary of the Navy that action be taken to render the dangerous ordnance harmless. Following up the Senator's letter, a team of Navy

The forward 30 feet of *U-352*'s bow is broken with a down angle of 30°. Gaping torpedo tube in center contains a destroyed torpedo. Photo by Tom Roach.

Senator Lowell Weicker (R-Conn.), a certified scuba diver, addressed a request to the Secretary of the Navy that action be taken to render *U-352*'s dangerous ordnance harmless. Courtesy of Senator Weicker.

divers conducted their own investigation in May, 1979. The 19 divers confirmed all that had been reported and that the other torpedoes still in the U-boat represented additional danger.

The internal investigation had been long and tedious. The forward torpedo room was 75% filled with sand and silt; the next compartment aft was 35% filled. Divers used airlift and peri-jet equipment to remove the sand and debris in order to determine whether any torpedoes or exploders were in the compartments. Next, the torpedo tube doors were drilled and probes were inserted into the tubes to determine whether they were loaded. Two of the four tubes did and still do contain torpedoes.

The aft torpedo room presented a similar problem except that there was no need to drill the torpedo tube door. The 2.5 feet of torpedo protruding outside the U-boat answered the question.

Several months passed without action by the Navy, but Senator Weicker was not to be denied. In October, 1979, he repeated his request that the ordnance be rendered harmless before an accidental death mandated corrective action. The Navy responded that they would do whatever was necessary as soon as climatic conditions would permit.

Three teams of Navy divers from Explosive Ordnance Disposal Group Two, Fort Story, Virginia, returned to *U-352* in May, 1980. Over a period of three weeks, more than 360 hours were spent on the bottom. The divers removed many 88mm shells and a torpedo warhead that was lodged under the deck framing. The torpedo extending from the stern tube was X-rayed to determine if it was armed. X-ray was also used on the torpedo wedged under the U-boat, partly buried in sand. Seven torpedoes in the forward torpedo room, including two inside torpedo tubes were not touched because they were deemed safe as long as they could be restricted from access.

Dave Bluett attaches a lift bag to *U-352* artifact forward of the conning tower. Photo by Jon Hulburt.

Navy divers returned to *U-352* in June, 1981 to install such a restriction. They spent nine days disarming the two torpedoes outside the U-boat. During the process, an accident occurred — the kind that had been feared. The exploder attached to the warhead of the stern tube torpedo detonated. Fortunately, the 600 pounds of explosives did not ignite and no injuries occurred.

U.S. Navy diver using an MK12 surface-supplied diving rig inspects a torpedo not equipped with an exploder. As a safety precaution exploders were not installed until torpedoes were ready for firing. Courtesy of U.S. Navy.

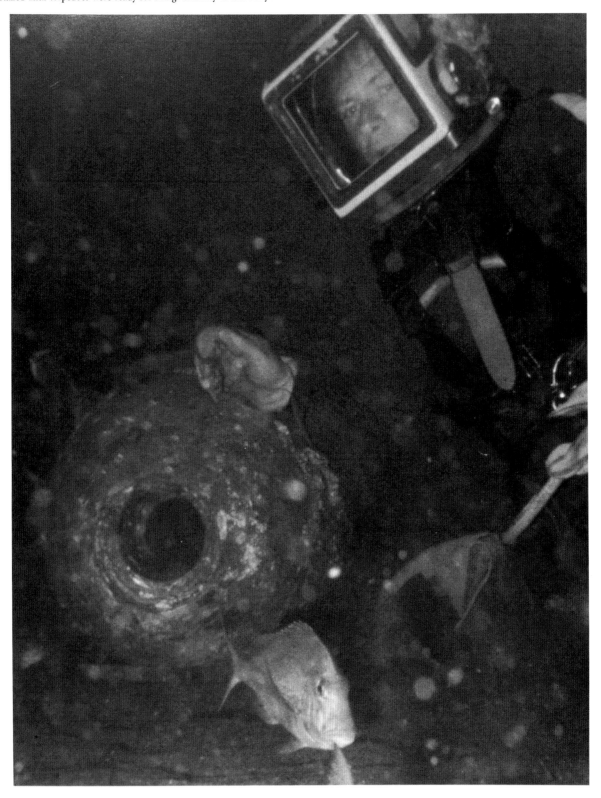

A torpedo protruding from the stern tube. A four pronged exploder is attached to the warhead. Courtesy of U.S. Navy.

U.S. Navy diver sends a lift bag to the surface with a torpedo warhead attached. Courtesy of U.S. Navy.

Steel plates were then installed over the five entrances to the interior to prevent access to all torpedoes and exploders inside the U-boat.

Within a few months, sport divers undid what had been fought for by the Senator. Two of the steel plates were removed, one covering the entrance to the forward torpedo room. What will the Navy's next action be? If the site cannot be made to remain safe will the government have it destroyed? At what cost? Apart from the expense of a demolition project, sport divers will have lost a superb diving experience, charter boats and fishermen will lose income, an historic site will be lost, and *U-352* will, once and for all, be lost in obscurity. In addition, the fate of every sunken U-boat or warship off the eastern seaboard may

be affected. If one U-boat must be demolished to assure the safety of divers, what reason is there to expect that all the others can be made safe without their destruction? And as they disappear, so do the artificial reefs that encourage marine growth in a meaningful contribution to underwater ecology. Such reefs are the purpose of dumping thousands of yards of rubble into waters off the east coast. What a waste to blast one into oblivion and pay for the construction of another.

The fate of *U-352* is in the balance. But, for a short while, her unproductive role in World War II has been overshadowed by a new glory. Through her rediscovery and accessibility, her remains have generated attention and debate, elevating her fame above the killer U-boats of her

U-352's open conning tower hatch, later removed by a scuba diver. Photo to Tom Roach.

U-352's conning tower sealed with a steel plate by U. S. Navy divers. Photo by H. Keatts.

era, *U-37* and *U-99*. More than 40 years after her launching, *U-352* has achieved in passive repose the public recognition that eluded her during her less than illustrious six-month wartime career.

But, fame is fleeting, and only time, scuba divers, and the United States Navy will determine how much longer *U-352* will enjoy it.

Steel plate removed from the conning tower by a scuba diver. Photo by H. Keatts.

Chuck Boswell joins another diver exploring the forward torpedo room. Photo by Jon Hulburt.

CHAPTER SEVEN

U-701 — SKY VICTIM

Two elderly couples came together by pre-arrangement at Lüneburg, a small West German village near the port of Hamburg in July, 1982. It was the first time they had met socially, but they were to spend the next week together in what is surely the most unusual reunion of World War II veterans on record.

It was the 40th anniversary of the sinking of the German U-boat, *U-701*. The men, one American, the other German, both grandfathers and retired, were Harry J. Kane, Jr., and Horst Degen. On July 7, 1942, 2nd Lieutenant Kane, then flying for the United States Army, had sunk Kapitän-leutnant Degen's U-boat with aerial depth charges off the coast of North Carolina.

The unprecedented reunion of victor and vanquished stemmed from an obscure newspaper account of another sunken German U-boat, *U-352*. United States Senator Lowell P. Weicker (R.-Conn.), an experienced scuba diver, had discovered a substantial amount of unexploded ordnance on a dive to the wreck. He recognized that uncontrolled accessibility to such potent explosives posed a serious safety hazard to the sport divers who frequented the site. His well-intended efforts to get the U.S. Navy to block entry to the U-boat raised heated controversy between divers and non-divers regarding the interests of sport divers. Many of the more persistent divers vowed to remove any bar to their entry. The media coverage of the story came to Kane's attention, and stimulated his interest in learning whether sport divers were visiting his World War II victim, *U-701*. Kane's investigation revealed that the U-boat had not only never been visited by sport divers, it had never even been located after

sinking. His interest fully aroused, he determined to do all he could to locate the wreck. His advantage lay in the fact that he had been at the site; that provided him with at least a general idea of where the vessel lay. He soon learned that more specific data would be needed if *U-701* was to be located. His futile search then drove him in another direction. One other who had been at the scene might be able to help, the commander of the lost U-boat.

A German newspaper provided Kane with the address of former Kapitänleutnant Degen. Correspondence followed, but to no avail. Neither he nor Degen, nor even their composite memories, could fix the location of the lost U-boat. Official records had proven to be in conflict and were of little use. Kane gave up the search without achieving his objective, but the long series of letters with Degen had established a close relationship between the American and the German. That bond set the stage for the 40 year reunion in Germany. There, in Degen's home-town, Kane greeted his one time enemy with a military salute. Both men introduced their wives, exchanged social pleasantries, and inevitably drifted into conversation about their war.

Later, Kane described the meeting. Degen, he observed, displayed only friendship — with no signs of animosity for Kane's role in the sinking of his U-boat. That was reaffirmation of what Degen had written in the series of letters between the two. Both men had performed their duties. They had been enemies at war, but for the week in July, 1982 they were old friends enjoying a wonderful vacation together, with their wives, on German soil. World War II, its death, destruction,

The adversaries meet again: former commander of *U-701*, Horst Degen (on left), and former bomber pilot Harry Kane discuss their fateful encounter, 40 years after sinking of *U-701*. Courtesy of Harry Kane.

U-boats, and bombers were a distant, imprecise memory except for their single common interest, Germany's *U-701*.

THE U-BOAT

The U-boat that brought the men together was a type VII-C, a 220-foot sleek war machine that carried two deck guns, 16 torpedoes, and a crew of 43. She was the first U-boat to be built by the firm of Stülcken Sohn Shipyard at Hamburg, Germany. That accounted for the early production problems that hindered her construction. Com-

pletion took more than a year, an unusually long time in those days. Her crew was assigned and ordered to Hamburg in March, 1941 to observe the final phases of construction and her launching in April.

The command of *U-701* was assigned on July 6, 1941 to Kapitänleutnant Horst Degen, naval class of 1933. While he was still a naval cadet, he had completed a round-the-world cruise that included the United States aboard the German cruiser, *Karlsruhe*. Degen, writing to the authors, recalled:

> The only place in the United States we were not cheered was Tacoma, Washington. Anti-Nazi leaflets had been scattered at the docks and around the city!! So we became first confronted with that problem of being a Nazi-sailor. We couldn't help it unless we became deserters . . . but we didn't anticipate what was going to happen until 1945!!!!

When Degen's naval application was approved in November 1932, his school director, Dr. Muller, had certified that the applicant was not a member of the Nazi party. That made the Tacoma incident particularly difficult for the young non-Nazi cadet. He had no control over the conflict in ideologies of the two countries, but his allegiance belonged to Germany. When war erupted, he served in Germany's Norwegian campaign as Torpedo and Radio Officer aboard the destroyer, *Hans Lody*. In 1940 he transferred to Kiel to attend the U-boat Commander School. During that training, Degen served board *U-552* for a one month war cruise under a daring leader, Kapitänleutnant Erich Topp, whose bold tactics exerted a lasting influence on the new U-boat

U-boat Acceptance Commission trials revealed a startling amount of construction faults in *U-701*. The U-boat is shown here in the Stülcken Shipyard for repair of some of those deficiencies. Courtesy of WZ-Bilddienst, Wilhelmshaven, West Germany.

commander.

Degen was ordered to assume command of *U-701* at Hamburg and sail her to Kiel for trials under the U-boat Acceptance Commission. The checkouts revealed a startling amount of faulty construction: electrical circuits were incorrectly wired and many air and fuel lines leaked because of improper fitting, all evidence of the shipyard's early production problems. The U-boat returned to Hamburg on August 3, 1941 for six weeks of corrective refitting. Then she returned to Kiel for completion of trials, including tests of her 88mm deck gun and 20mm anti-aircraft gun. Two weeks of torpedo practice followed at Warnemunde, where a close relationship developed between the U-boat crew and the members of the local rowing club. Before *U-701* departed, the club's pennant device, a red sea robin, was painted on her conning tower to link the rowing club and the citizens of Warnemunde with the destiny of the new U-boat.

Life as a U-boat commander suited Degen well. He was liked and respected by his crew and, in his own words, would have been only one of many officers of equal rank on a surface ship — but on the U-boat, he was his own master. Degen began to reflect what he had learned of "Commander Instructor" Topp's tactical philosophy during the

Kapitänleutnant Erich Topp, the daring leader whose bold tactics made a lasting impression on Horst Degen. Topp scored heavily along America's eastern seaboard. His total for the war was 33 ships and one submarine for 193,684 tons, making him Germany's third highest scoring U-boat ace. Like Degen, he survived the war. Courtesy of National Archives.

Kapitänleutnant Horst Degen gives the military salute at *U-701*'s ready for action ceremony (commissioning) at Stülcken Shipyard, Hamburg.

The sea robin insignia of *U-701*. Most U-boats carried an emblem, though about half carried the insignia of the flotilla rather than an individual emblem such as *U-701*'s. In some instances both were carried. Courtesy of Horst Degen.

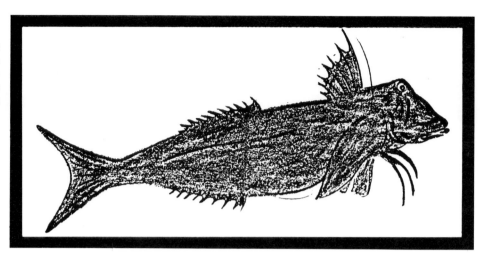

To Prof. Henry Keatts

Horst Degen

Feb. 10. 1985

Kapitänleutnant Horst Degen two months before his last mission. His white cap is adorned with a sea robin, his U-boat's insignia. Courtesy of Horst Degen.

The gun-crew fires *U-701*'s 88mm deck gun during a gunnery drill in 1941 while Degen and other officers observe the results through binoculars. Courtesy of Horst Degen.

short war cruise aboard *U-522*. Topp's fatalistic credo was an over-simplified belief that life is a matter of luck, and the odds in favor of success are no way enhanced by extreme caution. Many other U-boat commanders were apprehensive about travelling on the surface, or even at periscope depth, where they might be spotted from the air. Like Topp, Degen preferred to take his chance on the surface to spot potential victims, relying on alert lookouts to warn of danger.

FIRST WAR CRUISE

After technical exercises with nine other U-boats, *U-701* returned to Hamburg in mid-November for readjustments and overhaul. Then she proceeded to Kiel to load fuel and torpedoes. On December 27, 1941, with the United States now a combatant, the U-boat left Kiel on her first war cruise, to cover the northwest approaches to England.

The new U-boat passed through the Kiel Canal, and steered a course northward around England en route to Newfoundland. Violent gales swept *U-701*, making it impossible to launch any type of offensive action. While rounding England, *U-701* suffered her first casualty — First Watch Officer Weinitschke. Kapitänleutnant Degen reported in a letter to us that Weinitschke:

> ... was on watch during the night in a snowstorm. Suddenly he climbed from the conning tower to the deck to fasten some lid that clapped, but didn't take a rope for security and was instantly washed overboard. He had not told anybody what he was going to do. The neighboring look-out suddenly saw him step down the ladder. We tried to find him but couldn't. An appalling event ...

The U-boat continued on her mission after the search was abandoned. The loss of a fellow crew member is always depressing to those who remain. It was no exception for those aboard *U-701* until an unescorted freighter of about 3,500 tons was sighted in mid-January. *U-701* was about to engage in her first war action. Two torpedoes were fired, and the crew thrilled with pride at the news that both were hits. Degen watched the vessel sink; then he approached the survivors, by then in lifeboats, to learn the name of the vessel for his report. The survivors refused to respond to his questions and the U-boat left the area. Shortly later the area was swept by a strong gale heavy enough to swamp vessels much larger than the lifeboats. British sources later revealed that the freighter *Baron Erskine,* with her entire crew, was lost without trace in that area.

Early in February, with no further action to her credit, *U-701* headed for St. Nazaire to repair severe storm damages and construction faults that were discovered during the mission.

SECOND WAR CRUISE

The now seasoned U-boat left on her second war cruise early in March 1942. En route to his operational area off Seydis Fjord on the east coast of Iceland, Degen encountered four enemy vessels in four days. Two British armed trawlers,

The 3,500-ton freighter *Baron Erskine*, sent to the bottom in *U-701*'s first war action. Courtesy of The Mariners Museum, Newport News, Virginia.

Degen aboard *U-701* at the start of a war patrol. His white officer's cap identifies him as the U-boat commander. The binoculars around his neck were standard attire for U-boat lookouts, constantly on the alert for attack from the air. Courtesy of Horst Degen.

Notts County and *Steila Capella,* were sunk with one torpedo each. A single torpedo also dispatched a fish carrier, *Hengist,* to the bottom. Another armed trawler, *Angle,* was more fortunate. Degen's single torpedo missed, and the trawler escaped unharmed. The record of perfection — a hit for each torpedo fired — was shattered, but four of the five vessels *U-701* had attacked on her first two missions now lay on the bottom. Heavy seas severely hampered the U-boat in her patrol off Iceland. Although there were enemy ships to be sighted, Degen could not maneuver into attack position. One unproductive day followed another until, low on fuel, the U-boat set course for France. Instead of St. Nazaire, which was heavily damaged by a British Commando raid on March 27, Degen headed for Brest. *U-701* reached that port on April 15 and remained there for one month before refueling at Lorient for her next mission.

FINAL WAR CRUISE

On May 20, 1942, *U-701* left Lorient for the American coast on what was to be her last mission. Her five torpedo tubes were loaded — with three mines each. The assigned mission was to mine the busy entrance of the harbor at Norfolk, Virginia. The Atlantic crossing took three weeks during heavy seas, operating at slow speed to conserve fuel. Degen sacrificed valuable time just beyond mid-point when he spotted a

A relaxed moment for Degen, white cap, and other *U-701* crew-members in 1942. Courtesy of Horse Degen.

Degen inspecting his crew just before *U-701* departed the French port of St. Nazaire for her second war cruise. Courtesy of Horst Degen.

Degen, between cruises at La Baule, France, in front of Hotel St. Nazaire. Courtesy of Horst Degen.

A crewmember bundles up against the searing cold on the ice-encrusted *U-701* off Newfoundland, January 1942. Courtesy of Horst Degen.

potential victim, an eastbound passenger liner. At the expense of more than a day, he stalked the vessel to confirm that it was a legitimate target. When he approached close enough for identification, he learned to his chagrin that it was the *Drottningholm,* a Swedish liner carrying Axis diplomats from New York to Portugal. Degen had been informed of the ship and its free passage status, but it took hours of cautious approach to get close enough to read the designation "Diplomat" painted on her side. With critical operating hours of fuel wasted, the original course was resumed. Several days later a 15,000-ton British liner was sighted, but her speed quickly took her out of range, and *U-701* continued across the Atlantic. If an attack on either vessel had been possible, the mines would have been removed from their storage in the torpedo tubes.

Degen displayed uncharacteristic caution as he remained submerged approaching the American coast. The wisdom of his departure from form was driven home on June 12 when the U-boat surfaced and was spotted by aircraft. The lookout's alarm precipitated a four man plunge into the conning tower as *U-701* shot under the surface. The crash dive had reached only 40 feet when depth charges detonated alongside the hull, rocking the U-boat in a rigid test of her endurance. The lighting system failed, and the glass lenses of the control room gauges shattered, but there were no injuries, and only minor damage was inflicted.

The following night *U-701* fulfilled her mission. Degen used the lighthouses at Cape Henry and at Cape Charles as coordinates to guide him in planting his fifteen magnetic mines at the harbor entrance. The mines were equipped with pre-set timers to allow the U-boat to vacate the area before the mines could be detonated. An Allied convoy from Key West proved their effectiveness two days later with the sinking of the British armed trawler, *Kingston Ceylonite* and heavy damage to two tankers. The first ship to strike a mine was torn by a tremendous explosion, creating the initial impression that a U-boat had torpedoed the ship. The other vessels increased speed and adopted zig-zag courses, effective evasive action against torpedoes, but disastrous in a mine field. Almost immediately, two other ships were ripped by explosion. Two days later, the ore carrier S.S. *Santora* struck another mine and sank. Fortunately, although four Allied ships were sunk or damaged, only one merchant seaman was lost. Several days later, Degen and his crew received a coded message from Admiral Karl Dönitz congratulating them on their outstanding accomplishment.

While surfaced during the night of June 15, *U-701* received radio orders to remain submerged by day. The increased diligence of American anti-submarine forces had already cost Admiral Dönitz two U-boats, *U-85* and *U-352.* Degen headed offshore for deeper water before daylight. He tried to set the U-boat on the bottom at 150 feet, and later at 270 feet. But the vessel bounced along the bottom, carried by the heavy current of the Gulfstream. Even filling the ballast tanks had no effect. The grating sound of the U-boat being pushed over the sand bottom was audible on board the *U-701* through the sensitive underwater listening system that was used to pick up the

In calm seas, the narrow deck and conning tower of *U-701* offered a welcome change from the fetid atmosphere within. This photograph was taken in 1941. Later in the war the threat of aircraft made this a dangerous respite. Courtesy of Horst Degen.

beating of enemy ship propellers long before their mastheads appeared on the horizon. Degen reasoned that Allied surface patrols might be equally well equipped with listening devices that would locate his scraping U-boat. He lifted off the bottom to eliminate that risk and to avoid hull damage.

The following day two torpedoes were fired at an 8,000-ton freighter. Both missed, and the prey escaped. Degen surfaced off Cape Hatteras the following night — directly into the signal light challenge of a U.S. Coast Guard cutter. Quickly, the U-boat dissolved into the darkness before the cutter could engage it in action. The next day Degen sighted what he took to be the same cutter escorting a tanker and a freighter. Out of position for attack, he submerged, but only after the U-boat had been sighted. As soon as the two escorted vessels were safely out of range, the cutter returned to drop depth charges. It was a futile gesture. The U-boat escaped unscathed.

The next night, June 19, U-701 surfaced about 20 miles off Cape Hatteras, and Degen spotted what he was convinced was the same Coast Guard cutter he had seen twice before. It was a dark and misty night, making positive identification difficult, but those conditions were ideal for the German submarine. It drew to within 150 feet of the vessel's stern, both deck guns manned. Without warning, the U-boat opened with punishing fire. Only machine guns and small arms fire responded; the cutter's three-inch gun was inoperative because of a faulty firing spring. Shells were pumped into the helpless cutter until the American vessel lay dead in the water. Within 15 minutes the cutter, ablaze along its entire length, was convulsed by violent explosions as the flames penetrated its most volatile areas. The U-boat approached to within 90 feet and found no evidence of survivors. Unobserved by the Germans, the crew of the cutter, YP-389, had slipped over the side in life jackets. They were rescued four hours later by other cutters responding to their distress call. U-701 applied the coup de grace with 88mm shells to open massive holes in the cutter's waterline. United States Coast Guard cutter YP-389 quietly sank from sight at 34°57' N, 75°22' W.

Several days elapsed without further action until Degen sighted a convoy, but the U-boat could not intercept it. Another convoy was sighted on June 27, with better results. Two torpedoes were fired at the 6,985-ton British tanker, *Freedom*. One missed, but the other hit aft, damaging the vessel — not enough to sink her, but badly enough to force her return to Norfolk. American destroyers retaliated in a furious attack on the U-boat, which by that time had submerged. Depth charges shattered glass gauge lenses and crippled electric motors, but the damage was quickly repaired. That night the U-boat re-surfaced and two torpedoes were transferred below deck from their upper deck storage containers. The procedure was difficult and

Captain Degen shouts instructions from the bridge to his gun crew as they fire on YP-389. Courtesy of Harris Publications, Inc.

dangerous because *U-701* lacked the runners that were installed for that purpose on later models.

The next day, June 28, 1942, Degen sank his last ship, a large tanker escorted by a formidable force of two Coast Guard cutters and three aircraft. He assessed the numbers and punitive power of the escort, then approached to a distance of 3,000 feet and fired two torpedoes at the prime target. The navigator counted off the seconds as Degen anguished in uncertainty "Endless seconds . . . waiting . . . waiting . . . a miss?" He had already committed his U-boat to punishment by the escorts and was not to be denied. He turned to order another torpedo launched. As he did, the U-boat shuddered under the impact of a tremendous explosion that had the crew clutching for balance at one another, any handhold, or even the air. Degen peered incredulously through the attack periscope. A huge geyser erupted where one torpedo had struck amidships. Fire swept the length of the fuel-laden tanker with ferocious intensity as Degen signaled nearby crewmen to take turns at the periscope for a quick view of the spectacle before the U-boat crash dived.

Patterns of depth charges saturated the area, but *U-701* and her daring commander were spared once again. Degen had accepted the challenge confronted with overwhelming odds — and had earned a major victory. *U-701* had not merely survived the attack, she was not even damaged. There could be no more convincing support for the German commander's doctrine of predestination. Clearly, his time had not yet arrived, and when it did, neither caution nor circumstances would influence the result.

Although the tanker had suffered grave damage, all 50 of her crew were rescued by the escort vessels. That night, eleven hours after the initial attack, the U-boat surfaced, and delivered the coup de grace with one more well-placed torpedo. Degen invited many of the crew to join him on the bridge to observe the action. Less than a minute after the torpedo struck, the tanker started down by the stern, flaming bow upright, as though reaching for the sky — an inquisitory torch probing the darkness. The sinking was slow, almost deliberate, until the bow followed into the depths to the hissing accompaniment of boiling seawater. Then, silence.

Awed seamen returned to their stations, the U-boat left the scene, and Degen referred to a 1940 British publication *Merchant Ships* to identify his latest sinking. It seemed to be the 12,000-ton *Gulfpride*. He radioed the news to German headquarters, elated over the size of his victim. The vessel was later confirmed to be an even larger vessel, the 14,057-ton tanker, *William Rockefeller,* carrying 125,000 barrels of oil. *U-701* had indeed done well.

The days that followed were uneventful except for frequent aircraft alarms whenever the U-boat surfaced to ventilate. The air-filtering system was out of order, and the foul air, high temperature, and high humidity produced nausea, headaches, and overall misery. The most effective way to clear the atmosphere was to surface, open the conning tower hatch, block all other air inlet valves, and run the diesels. The engines drew in all the contaminated air for combustion, creating a powerful draft in the conning tower and throughout the boat. Temporarily purified with fresh air, the U-boat would submerge until the need arose again.

Captain Degen invited members of the crew to view the tanker's final minutes. Courtesy of Harris Publications, Inc.

The 14,057-ton tanker *William Rockefeller*, sunk by *U-701*. The tanker's entire 50-man crew was rescued by escort vessels. Tankers were prime targets for U-boats as their cargo was vital for the Allied war effort. Courtesy of The Mariners Museum, Newport News, Virginia.

The frequent need for ventilation during daylight hours placed a heavy demand on the lookouts. Degen, himself, served as a lookout, as did his executive officer Oberleutnant zur See Konrad Junker. On the morning of July 7, 1942, Degen reprimanded Junker for his failure to spot a plane sooner. That afternoon, Junker would acknowledge responsibility of the loss of *U-701* and most of her crew. Forty-three years later, Degen's only indictment of his subordinate was that he was a "drowsy lookout."

THE SINKING

The U-boat surfaced to ventilate at 1:00 P.M. at a location where only a few miles to the east the depth dropped off abruptly to several thousand feet. Degen later described the site to be less than 200 feet deep — a critical difference between the certainty of death and the possibility of survival in case of a sinking. But his thoughts were not on the problems of getting off the bottom as he, Junker, and two others assumed their lookout stations, each covering a sector of 90 degrees. Scanning the skies with their binoculars, each distant seagull could have been hostile aircraft to the tense Germans. Then unobserved, a U.S. Army bomber on routine anti-submarine patrol out of the Marine Corps air station at Cherry Point, N.C., detected the U-boat and approached, protected by cloud cover. It was almost on top of the Germans before Junker awoke to it presence. He hysterically sounded the alert, and *U-701* crash dived to the echo of his "Airplane, there!"

"You saw it too late," an exasperated Degen criticized as the U-boat struggled to gain the safety of depth. His executive officer nodded a shamed acknowledgement an instant before the American plane attacked from the stern at an altitude of only 50 feet. Only 15 or 20 seconds after submergence, three 315-pound depth charges were dropped on the U-boat. The first fell short, but the next two straddled the submarine. Encapsulated between the two tremendous explosions, the pressure hull was torn open and water swept into the stern, through the engine room, and into the control room. The ballast tanks were blown immediately in a desperate effort to re-surface, but it was too late. *U-701* was on her way to the bottom.

Degen later wrote of the sinking: "The instruments showed 60 meters (195 feet) when, with a light bounce, our mortally wounded submarine was thrown to the bottom of the ocean." The U-boat settled on an even keel, then listed about 30 degrees to starboard. Degen and those with him in the control room were cut off at once from the other compartments by the rapidly rising seawater. In the short interval since the attack, the water level had risen to within a foot of the control room ceiling. In the dim emergency lighting, Degen ordered his men to follow as he opened the conning tower hatch cover — and was catapulted 200 feet to the surface by the released air pressure. Sixteen followed him in a column of air bubbles.

The bomber, piloted by 2nd Lieutenant Harry Kane, Jr., remained in the area, circling in a search for evidence to support the claim of a

The numbers on this illustration, redrawn from Lt. Kane's attack analysis, represent the paths and explosions of the three depth charges dropped on *U-701*.

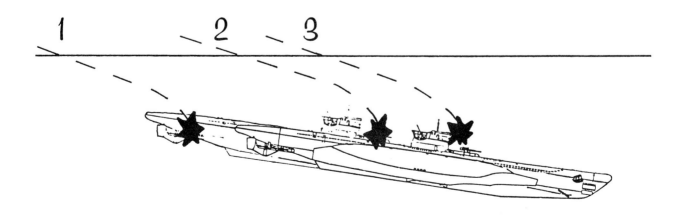

Lockheed-Hudson bomber of the type flown by Lt. Kane when he caught *U-701* on the surface and destroyed her with depth charges. Courtesy of National Archives.

U-boat sunk. There was much turbulence, but little debris. Then, the sea was dotted with survivors popping through the surface, most without life preservers. Without regard for the risk to him and his crew, Kane ordered all life preservers and the only life raft aboard to be dropped. Only one of the life preservers was retrieved by a survivor. The others and the raft drifted away, untouched — the difference between life and death for many of those struggling for survival. Unable to provide additional equipment, the plane circled the area for another hour as the German sailors drifted off, borne by the strong Gulfstream current.

After 30 minutes, a second group of 18 men escaped from *U-701*'s forward torpedo room. They had managed to secure the water-tight door leading to their compartment, ahead of the rising water. The torpedo loading hatch offered the only chance for them to escape certain death. One after another they squeezed through, and surfaced to an uncertain freedom. Lieutenant Kane, still circling overhead, was totally frustrated by the sudden appearance of the new survivors. He had no equipment to offer, and his fuel was running dangerously low. Then he sighted a nearby Panamanian freighter, and signaled for it to pick up the Germans. The freighter acknowledged the message before the plane left for refueling — but the survivors went unaided. Influenced by dis-

cretion, the Panamanian ship continued on its course, for fear that the U-boat might still be operational — and the floating seamen drifted away on the current.

Kane had directed rescue craft to the site of the sinking, but they arrived to find no sign of survivors or debris. When Kane returned to his base at Cherry Point Air Station, North Carolina, his claim of a "kill" was greeted by derision and disbelief. Without supporting evidence, he and his crew were considered in the class of others who had reported sinking U-boats — sinkings that were later discredited.

THE ORDEAL

Degen was confident of quick rescue for his group of 17, particularly with the continued presence of the American bomber over the attack area. Confidence gave way to concern as the persistent current carried the survivors away from the sinking. Most were without life preservers — five at one time sharing a single preserver. Within 30 minutes, two non-swimmers had choked on so much seawater that the others could no longer keep them afloat. They slipped away, and the small cluster was reduced to 15.

Two others later succumbed to exhaustion. Both had been injured; one with a fractured leg, the other with a gaping head wound. Now they were gone and only 13 remained.

Lt. Harry Kane points to the position off the coast of North Carolina, where he and his crew (left to right) Cpl. G.E. Bellamy, Cpl. P.C. Broussard, 2nd Lt. L.A. Murray, and Cpl. L.P. Flowers sank *U-701*. Courtesy of U.S. Naval Historical Center.

The day wore on without promise of rescue until it became evident that none would come that day. They would have to try to stay afloat through the terror of darkness that would screen them from any possibility of rescue. Near sundown, Junker, the errant lookout, and one of the crewmen decided to take off on their own. They struck out toward land, which they knew lay to the west, using the setting sun for guidance. They hoped to reach the superstructure of a shipwreck that had been observed just before the air attack, but they were never heard of again. Only 11 of the 17 remained.

The survivors drifted for a second day under a punishing sun. Parched and swollen, cracked lips and constricted throats begged for relief, but the seawater only worsened matters. The weaker succumbed to fatigue, dehydration, or drowning. Incredibly, not all perished; some hung on with desperate tenacity. Degen, himself, lay unconscious on the surface for long intervals, kept afloat only by the combined efforts of three of his crew who took turns keeping his head above water.

Hope of rescue soared at about noon of the second day as a U.S. Coast Guard vessel was sighted. It was headed directly for the German sailors until it changed direction and veered away at about 3,000 feet from the frantic calls and flailing arms. Bobbing heads and waving hands were lost in the two to four-foot ocean swells. Hope dwindled as the American ship disappeared, and the persistent drift continued to carry the lost survivors along the northeast current to — who knew where?

Another night screened the exhausted derelicts from any prospect of rescue. They had been in the water for over 30 hours, without food, water, or rest — most of the time under a brutal sun. Resistance was low, and all action was either by reflex or instinct. Still, they drifted on the mercifully warm current, minds numbed — like zombies in all but the waning hope that somehow they would survive. There was always the fear of predatory sea animals to maintain an alert watch through the darkness, though any form of resistance would have been out of the question. No marauding attacks developed, perhaps because the weakened sailors who slipped away in silent death during the ordeal were sufficient for unseen scavengers, willing to wait a little longer for the rest.

Suddenly, out of the darkness, a symbol of salvation took form, borne on the same contradictory Gulfstream that supported them and provided warmth while at the same time it carried them away from rescue. A lemon and a coconut came bobbing to within reach and were quickly snared by the survivors. Not much nourishment for 11 famished sailors, with parched throats and puckered lips to be taunted by the lemon, and the hard coconut shell to test their ability to break through.

The lemon posed little problem, except to provide for an equal distribution. It was torn in half, to be passed from man to man, each taking a taste. Its food value was little, but it helped — perhaps in morale more than anything else. According to Degen, "It burned like Hell in our throats but gave some stimulus." The coconut offered both milk and meat, but only if it could be opened. Several days before the sinking, the elastic in Degen's swim trunks had stretched, and he had pulled the waistband tighter with a safety pin. Using that safety pin, the men took turns boring two holes, through which each had a refreshing swallow of coconut milk. Then they attacked the shell with the sharp edge of the release handle from an escape lung compressed air bottle.

The sailors ravenously attacked the coconut meat — but only at the greatest discomfort. With nostrils swollen almost closed from saltwater, they had to breathe through their mouths. Their efforts to chew the meat and breathe at the same time had them choking, gasping for breath, and swallowing seawater. Shreds of coconut meat trapped at the juncture of throat and windpipe added to the misery. Degen later recalled, "It was one of those desperate situations that has no parallel in normal daily activity, and it is impossible to imagine." The entire episode — from sinking to rescue might best be described by those words.

When dawn broke on July 9, 1942, only four of the original 17 who had escaped from the conning tower were still alive. As the day progressed, it differed in no way from the two that had preceded it — hot sun, endless expanse of seawater, no drink, no food, no rescue — hour after endless hour. Morning gave way to afternoon with no change — nothing but hot sun and endless sea. Then hearts skipped a beat as above the horizon, a United States Navy blimp took form, getting larger and larger as it approached. It was the Navy blimp *K-8*, the most beautiful object the survivors had ever seen. But could it, would it see them — tiny dots on a vast sea? Was it indeed real, or a mirage, only imagined?

The blimp was indeed real, and the four survivors had been sighted. Ensign G.S. Middleton, commanding, had located them at 36°18' N, 73°32' W, about 110 miles offshore — nearly 90 miles from where the U-boat was thought to have sunk. The miracle of locating them had been achieved by calculating the effect of a two-knot drift for 50 hours. A life raft was first dropped, then food, water, blankets, and a first-aid kit were lowered. The blimp signaled for a Coast Guard rescue seaplane, and remained overhead until it arrived. Fifty hours of traumatic misery had ended for the four survivors as they were loaded aboard the rescue plane.

When Degen was picked up by the seaplane, he was happily surprised to see three crewmen who had not escaped with him from the conning tower. They were the remaining survivors of the 18 who had escaped from the forward torpedo room. They had been plucked from the sea earlier by the rescue plane. A 15-mile area search produced only the bodies of five more crewmen, all dead in life preservers, and a number of empty life preservers.

All seven survivors were, by coincidence, unmarried. One, 19-year-old seaman Bruno Faust, had served aboard another U-boat, one that had been sunk with the loss of her entire crew less than three months earlier. Faust had missed the last cruise of that U-boat, *U-85*, when he developed a serious cold while in Lorient. When he recovered he was transferred to *U-701*, where he was to serve on her last cruise — but to survive.

PRISONERS OF WAR

Within three hours of their rescue, the dehydrated prisoners, exhausted and severely sun-

U-701 survivors cling to life raft dropped from U.S. Navy blimp, K-8. The burning smoke bomb identifies the location as the blimp hovers overhead. Courtesy of National Archives.

Werner Seldte, *U-701* Torpedo Specialist, swims to U.S. Coast Guard rescue seaplane — and survival. Courtesy of National Archives.

Four bewildered, oil-smeared, semi-nude *U-701* survivors wait to be helped aboard U.S. Coast Guard rescue plane. Courtesy of National Archives.

Horst Degen being carried ashore for transfer to U.S. Navy Hospital at Norfolk, Virginia. Courtesy of U.S. Naval Historical Center.

burned, were under military interrogation. Four were in swim trunks and three were naked, but all were thoroughly coated with a heavy layer of fuel that had spewed into the water from their U-boat. Without that protection they would have been burned to a crisp by the summer sun. In their weakened condition, the Germans proved to be less resistant to their captors' questions than under more normal conditions. Their resistance stiffened as they began to recover, and recognize the significance of the questions they were being asked. Although important information was divulged, no reference was made to *U-701*'s mine-laying mission to Norfolk. Only after the end of the war did the United States learn that mines, not torpedoes, were responsible for the devastation suffered by the convoy as it entered Norfolk Harbor.

Four days after the rescue, Kane's squadron commander ordered him to board a flight for the Norfolk Air Station with his crew: Navigator 2nd Lt. L.A. Murray, Bombardier Cpl. G.E. Bellamy, Radio Operator Cpl. L.P. Flowers, and Engineer Cpl. P.C. Broussard. They were greeted by a delegation of Naval officers and civilians, to be ceremoniously ushered into the Naval Hospital. Unusual security precautions prevailed. Non-uniformed agents, who might have been FBI, guarded the entrances with submachine guns cradled in their arms.

The bomber crew was led into an over-sized room to meet badly sunburned Kapitänleutnant Degen, who sat in a wheelchair dressed in a hospital robe. The significance of the moment struck Kane as he realized that the man with Degen was the Secretary of the Navy, Frank Knox. The airmen were congratulated for their achievement, and the U-boat captain was informed that these were the men who had destroyed *U-701*. When Kane was pointed out as the officer

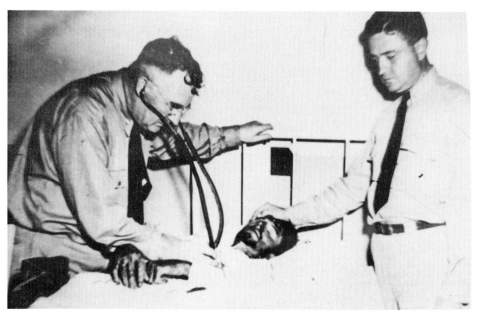

Exhausted from his ordeal in the sea, Degen is attended by U.S. Navy doctors on July 9, 1942, at the Navy Hospital at Norfolk, Virginia. Courtesy of National Archives.

Lt. Kane and his bomber crew meet Kapitänleutnant Degen of *U-701*, at the U.S. Navy Hospital on July 13, 1942, four days after Degen's rescue. Courtesy of National Archives.

in command, Degen rose from his wheelchair, snapped to attention with a military salute, and paid tribute to the American who had defeated him. "Congratulations," he praised. "Good attack." Defeat had not cost the German officer his dignity, nor did it cloud his assessment of a sound military action by his adversary.

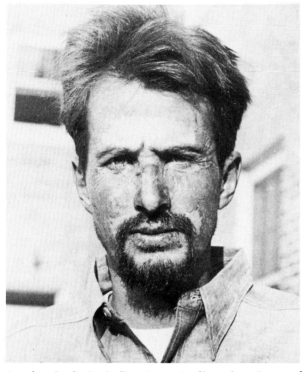

Degen's peeling forehead reflects the severity of his sunburn. Courtesy of Horst Degen.

The captured Germans were out of uniform when they were picked up, but there was no question that they were legitimate prisoners of war, not spies. They were transferred to Camp Blanding, Florida, where they remained for two years. Then the POW's were sent to Camp Papago Park near Phoenix, Arizona. After war ended, the survivors were returned to Germany. They were released at Hamburg on June 6, 1946. Two months later Degen married a war-widow with two sons, whose husband had been killed in action near Smolensk on the eastern front in 1943. On April 19, 1948, his wife Lotte presented Degen with his own son.

Degen reacted favorably to the treatment he had received during his four years as a prisoner of war. In a letter to the authors he observed:

> As POW's we had a fair, good, correct, and humane treatment. A thankful feeling towards the USA and 'Uncle Sam' is always going to stay in my heart!!

Five of *U-701*'s seven survivors are still alive in 1985. Bruno Faust and Gerhardt Schwendel, both Mechanikergefreiter (Seaman 2cl), live in East Germany. Herbert Grotheer, Funkmaat (Radioman 3cl), and Werner Seldte, Mechanikergefreiter (Seaman 2cl), live in West Germany and meet with Horst Degen in a reunion almost every year. Ludwig Vaupel, Machinemaat, referred to by Degen as his Control Room Chief, died in 1959. Gunter Kunert, Obersterumann (Navigator), died in 1966.

Lieutenant Kane received the Distinguished Flying Cross for his role in sinking *U-701*. After

U-701 survivors from left to right: Herbert Grotheer, Wireless Operator; Gerhardt Schwendel, Diesel Machinist; Ludwig Vaüpel, Control Room Machinist (died 1959); Werner Seldte, Torpedo Specialist; Gunter Kunert, Navigator (died 1966); Bruno Faust, Torpedo Specialist; Horst Degen, Commanding Officer. Courtesy of National Archives.

action in the Pacific against the Japanese, he served as a flight instructor until his retirement with the rank of Captain.

Ensign Middleton and the crew of the U.S. Navy blimp *K-8* received a letter of commendation for their rescue of the *U-701* survivors.

Kapitänleutnant Horst Degen's one year U-boat career accounted for eight vessels sunk, two by mines. For that short period, he lived by what he had learned from his U-boat instructor, Kapitänleutnant Erich Topp: "Life is a matter of luck, and the odds in favor of success are in no way enhanced by extreme caution." He had taken more than his fair share of risks, he had succeeded, and he had survived — living proof that Topp's fatalism worked. His command, *U-701,* and 36 of her crew were not so fortunate. Their remains are lost in the sea, somewhere off the Atlantic coast of North Carolina.

WRECK LOCATION

The interest of sport divers has been whetted by the possibility that *U-701* is at a reasonable depth for scuba diving. Several expeditions have searched for the U-boat, but no evidence has been advanced to indicate that they have been successful, despite rumors that she has been found.

The problem in locating the wreck is compounded by the number of positions reported in official documentation of the action. Navy records reflect a range of 49" latitude and 1°8" longitude as the following extracts, all from official sources, indicate:

POSITION

Latitude	Longitude	
34°50' N	— 74°55' W	...Lieutenant Kane's report
35°05' N	— 75°54' W	...Navy report listed best position available
34°24' N	— 75°11' W	...096 from Hatteras Light — Navy report
35°12' N	— 74°48' W	...096 from Cape Hatteras — Navy report
35°13' N	— 74°46' W	...36 miles SE of Cape Hatteras — Navy report
34°52' N	— 74°54' W	...Navy Report

One of the locations may be correct, or close — but which, if any? A degree of latitude measures about 70 miles. One degree of longitude at the indicated 34° or 35° latitude is about 45 miles. With a possible range of 49" latitude and 1°08" longitude, the search area would encompass more than 2,900 square miles — more than 40% larger than the State of Delaware. Any serious attempt to find *U-701* must be based on the more precise estimates.

U-boat Headquarters enclosure "A" to the log of *U-701* from the Submarine Force Library and Museum at Groton, Connecticut. All U-boats carried such grid covered charts (duplicates of those at U-boat Headquarters). The grid system allowed Admiral Dönitz to deploy his U-boats without fear of enemy interception of his orders. In turn the U-boats could keep headquarters informed of their locations without giving the information to the enemy. *U-701's* last reported position was CA 87. Courtesy of Submarine Force Library and Museum.

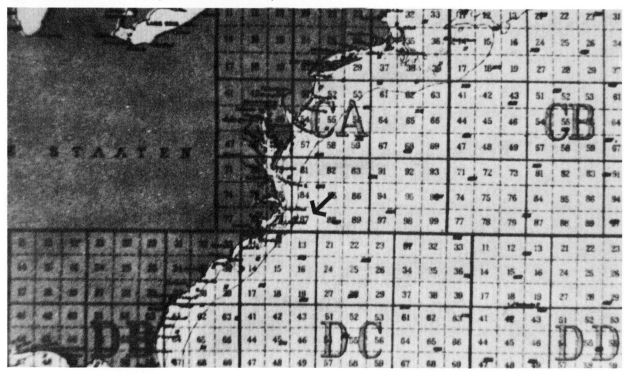

Scuba divers are intensely interested in finding the U-boat, but only if she lies within their diving depth range, no more than 250 feet. It may well be in that range, because Degen's reading was 195 feet as his vessel touched bottom. With fully flooded compartments, her 769-ton displacement might have been sufficient to resist even the strong drift of the two-knot Gulfstream current.

The discovery of *U-701* could depend upon chance, a snagged net, or a random depth recorder pattern. Or it may evolve from a carefully planned search based on recorded data, interviews, painstaking analysis — and some luck. In a 1983 interview, Kane declared to the authors that he sank *U-701* 24 miles due east of Avon, North Carolina. Other official Navy records put the location between 30 and 38 miles offshore. In either case, the depth at that point would be prohibitive for scuba divers. Fortunately for the hopes of sport divers, other evidence seems to favor a position closer to shore than either Kane's estimate or the Navy's official records.

Immediately before the sinking, in Degen's words, "Far in the west, against the distant shore, we could make out the funnel and the mastheads of a wreck . . ." Degen would have made such an observation from high on the conning tower of the surfaced U-boat. That would place him 12 to 18 feet above the water, depending on whether *U-701* was riding high or with decks awash and also on Degen's level on the conning tower deck. Assuming he was as much as 18 feet above sea level, his range of sight at Kane's estimate of 24 nautical miles offshore would have been limited to objects (a shoreline or mastheads) at least 280 feet high (See Appendix F for range of sight formula). But Hatteras Island is a barrier strip, not even a hilly shore.

Both Degen and Kane were at the scene, and their descriptions are contradictory. If Degen is credited with having seen ". . . the distant shore," and that shore was no more than 25 or 50 feet above sea level, the distance was somewhere between 10 and 13 miles. Assuming that range instead of Kane's 24 miles offshore estimate or the Navy's 30 to 38 miles, reduces the search area by two-thirds. Degen's credibility is enhanced by his reading of 195 feet (60 meters) as *U-701* touched

bottom. Nautical charts of the area show that the floor of the sea off Avon drops to 1,000 feet approximately 25 miles offshore.

The information provided by Lieutenant Kane should be reliable. After all, he headed the crew that sank the U-boat, logged the location, and radioed directions to rescue craft. However, it may be significant that the rescue craft failed to find evidence of the sinking when they arrived. It is of course possible that the strong Gulfstream current carried off all signs of the sinking before the rescue vessels arrived on the scene.

If Kane was correct in his estimate that the sinking occurred due east of Avon, North Carolina, the search area would be narrowed appreciably. Combined with Degen's observation regarding the distance offshore, searchers might have a reasonable chance of finding the U-boat. However, unless the official Navy records reflect a glaring typographical error, Kane's radioed position was nowhere near Avon, nor even Hatteras Island when he came upon *U-701*. Those records report his position as 34°50' N — 74°55' W, more than 43 nautical miles southeast of Avon and 74 nautical miles east of Atlantic, North Carolina. If Kane was indeed east of Avon at the time of the sinking, and his radio directions were as recorded in Navy records, it might explain why responding rescue craft could find neither survivors nor debris. With all the confusion that shrouds her location, it is no wonder that *U-701* remains undiscovered.

Many clues tempt the curious. Further research may confirm or disprove them one by one. Recollections of ". . . the funnels and masthead of a wreck . . .," records of ocean bottom soundings to eliminate consideration of all areas more than 20 feet above or below 195 feet, interviews with local fishermen, plus a host of other channels invite investigation. Some item of information recorded in this chronicle of *U-701* may contribute to her ultimate discovery. If so, we would feel amply repaid with an invitation to photograph Kapitänleutnant Horst Degen's U-boat where she lies somewhere off the coast of North Carolina, beneath the warm waters of the Gulfstream current.

CHAPTER EIGHT

LAST KILL IN AMERICAN WATERS — U-853

The nautical chart of Rhode Island Sound features a circle, seven miles east of Block Island, R.I., labeled "Danger, unexploded depth charge, May 1945." That circle, cryptic monument to the last sea action between the U.S. and Nazi Germany, marks the sandy grave of German U-boat *U-853*. Her story tells of the end of a struggle for an ocean; her death tolls the knell for the end of a war.

By 1942, Germany's U-boats had come perilously close to their objective of controlling the major sea lanes of the Atlantic. Sinkings of Allied ships soared to 1,570 for a total of 7,697,000 tons. Germany's *U-123* alone sank six ships in 24 hours, contributing to the loss ratio of 40 Allied ships sunk to one U-boat destroyed during the first quarter of 1942.

Winston Churchill, wrote in *The Second World War:*

> The Battle of the Atlantic was the dominating factor all through the war. Never for one moment could we forget that everything happening on land, sea, and in the air depended ultimately on its outcome and amid all other cares we viewed its changing fortunes day by day with hope or apprehension.

During the 1942 period of euphoria for German submarine crews, the keel of *U-853* was laid. She was commissioned on June 25, 1943, under Kapitänleutnant Helmut Sommer, a U-boat commander for two years.

After commissioning, *U-853* spent the next few months on a shake-down cruise in the Baltic. Anxious and eager for action, the crew was blissfully unaware that the "Happy Time" was

over and the Battle of the Atlantic had already undergone dramatic reversal. In the last quarter of 1942, the Allied loss ratio dropped from forty-to-one to ten-to-one. By mid-1943, when *U-853* was commissioned, U-boats were being hunted down and methodically destroyed by Allied aircraft and destroyers. The new U-boat was to sail into a changed environment, a different battlefield.

U-853 was a Type IXC_{40} U-boat, 251'10" long, with a beam of 22'10", and 1,144 tons displacement. The design was essentially the same as the IXC model but with added communication and hydrophone equipment in a hull that was increased by 4" in beam to accommodate additional fuel. Her pressure hull was divided into six water-tight compartments by bulkheads with circular doors three feet in diameter. Armament consisted of four bow and two stern torpedo tubes, 22 torpedoes, one 37mm anti-aircraft gun with 2,625 rounds and four paired 20mm anti-aircraft guns with 8,000 rounds. Near the end of the war, far more ammunition was carried because of increased air attacks. Special water and pressure tight ammunition lockers were fitted into the deck next to the guns for ready access.

FIRST MISSION

On April 29, 1944, *U-853* left Kiel on her first war mission with a crew of four officers and 44 enlisted men. The U-boat made one stop in Norway before heading into the Atlantic, passing between Iceland and the Shetland Islands.

U-853 and four other U-boats had been assigned to the mid-Atlantic, between Newfoundland and

Commissioning of *U-853*. Kapitänleutnant Helmut Sommer is fifth from the right in the front row. Oberleutnant Helmut Frömsdorf is on his left. Courtesy of Fred Benson.

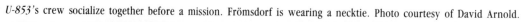

U-853's crew socialize together before a mission. Frömsdorf is wearing a necktie. Photo courtesy of David Arnold.

TYPE IXC₄₀

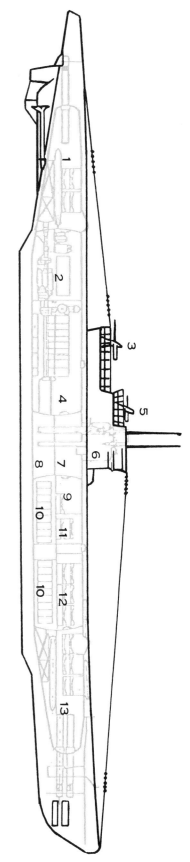

1. Aft torpedo room & crew quarters
2. Electric motor room
3. 37mm anti-aircraft gun
4. Diesel engine room
5. 20mm anti-aircraft gun
6. Conning tower
7. Control room

8. Sonar room
9. Radio room & commander's quarters
10. Batteries
11. Officer's quarters
12. Crew quarters
13. Forward torpedo room & crew quarters

Displacement (tons)	
Surfaced	1,144
Submerged	1,257
Length	251'10"
Beam	22'10"
Draught	15'6"
Fuel capacity (tons)	218
Speed (knots)	
Surfaced	18.25
Submerged	7.25
Range (nautical miles/kn.)	
Surfaced	14,353/10
Submerged	63/4
Armament	
Bow torpedo tubes	4
Stern torpedo tubes	2
Torpedoes carried (number/size)	22/21"
Guns (number/size)	2/20mm — 1/37mm
Crew	48

119

the Azores, to make weather observations for defense of the European Continent. With such information, German Intelligence believed it could anticipate Allied invasion plans across the English Channel, which would be influenced heavily by weather conditions.

En route to her weather post, *U-853* came upon a convoy. Two torpedoes were fired without success before the convoy's location was radioed to U-boat Headquarters.

Although the meterological mission was not as dangerous as attacking an escorted convoy, it was still risky. Each U-boat had a meterologist on board and had to surface daily for weather observations and to transmit the conditions by radio. Every message provided Allied units in the Atlantic with the opportunity for a radio-directional fix on the surfaced U-boat.

On May 25, *U-853* stumbled upon one of the most sought after targets in the Atlantic. Surfaced to transmit a weather report, Sommer sighted the gigantic profile of *Queen Mary* filling the horizon. Immediately, he ordered the U-boat in pursuit but the fast ocean liner easily outran *U-853*. Large ocean liners usually required no escort because they were so fast that no U-boat could get

U-853 entering a French port. The U-boat holds the dubious distinction of becoming the last U-boat to be sunk in American waters. Courtesy of Fred Benson.

into attack position unless she happened to be in the right spot to begin with, either by plan or coincidence.

U-853 surfaced to complete her interrupted weather transmission. Suddenly, three rocket-firing British planes roared down. They were Swordfishes from *Ancylus* and *MacKendrick*, M.A.C. (merchant aircraft catapault) ships fitted with a short flight deck, each capable of carrying up to five aircraft.

Instead of diving as expected, Sommer ordered his anti-aircraft gun crews into action. His daring strategy momentarily confused the attacking pilots. Then, while the three planes regrouped for a second attack, the Captain took *U-853* down to safety.

The U-boats were ordered to remain at their stations to provide the weather data that was deemed so valuable that the orders continued, even after D-day. Experience taught the U-boats that each broadcast triggered an attack. In reaction, they would dash to a new position after each weather report to the accompaniment of exploding depth charges.

On June 15, a Hunter-Killer group, the carrier *Croatan* and six destroyers, zeroed in on *U-853*. For 72 hours, aircraft from the carrier combed the area while the destroyers waited patiently, secure in the knowledge that eventually the U-boat would have to surface. Captain John P.W. Vest, commander of the *Croatan* group, drove his men so relentlessly that they named the elusive *U-853* "Moby Dick," after the great white whale that was pursued so passionately by Captain Ahab in Herman Melville's classic American novel.

During their exposure to the Hunter-Killer group, *U-853*'s crew bestowed their own name on their vessel, now a survivor of her first depth charge assault. In admiration for Sommer's skill in eluding the attackers, they affectionately named the U-boat "Der Seiltaenger" (The Tightrope Walker).

On June 18, still in pursuit, *Croatan*'s high-frequency direction-finder intercepted a weather transmission from *U-853*, only 30 miles distant. Within 11 minutes, fighter planes from the carrier were strafing the deck of the surfaced U-boat. This time the anti-aircraft gun crews were not so fortunate. Two were killed, the rest wounded. In all, 14 crewmen were wounded. Sommer, on the bridge, was riddled by slugs and fragments that ripped into his head, stomach, and arms. The Captain suffered 28 wounds, but stayed on his feet, directing the struggle to save his boat.

Fighter planes from USS *Croatan (CVE-25)* strafed *U-853*, killing two and wounding 14 including Captain Sommer. Courtesy of National Archives.

121

Fast behind the fighters came bomb-laden Avengers to finish off the U-boat. The bombers arrived just as the sea closed over the stricken *U-853*. The wounded Sommer had managed to submerge her in time.

Sommer knew the aerial attack would be followed with pursuit by the destroyers. Three tracked the sub by sonar as the U-boat appeared to start for her home port in Lorient, France, on the Bay of Biscay. Then, in a deceptive maneuver, Sommer headed off course. The ruse worked and *U-853* miraculously escaped almost certain destruction. She was reprieved to roam the seas for almost another year. Like Ahab, Captain Vest (of *Croatan*) had come tormentingly close to his prey but failed to exterminate her. Sommer and his 14 wounded crewmen recovered.

Much of the responsibility for returning *U-853* to her Lorient base fell on the shoulders of the 23-year-old Executive Officer, Oberleutnant Helmut Frömsdorf. Under Sommer's tutelage, Frömsdorf picked up valuable experience, which he would need later.

U-853 reached France on July 4, 16 days after the air attack. She underwent repairs and stood by for installation of a schnorchel, a retractable air intake and exhaust pipe invented by the Dutch, to permit operation of her diesel engines while submerged. The new device reduced the perilous periods on the surface for charging batteries.

U-853 did not get her schnorchel in Lorient because the Allies were advancing on that port city. She was the last U-boat to leave the base. On August 27, *U-853* left for Norway under Korvettenkapitän Gunter Kuhnke, commander of the 10th Flotilla.

The U-boat was equipped with her schnorchel in October, at a German shipyard, and was again ready for the Atlantic. The schnorchel provided additional security, but she still could not attack without exposure to effective reprisal.

SECOND AND FINAL MISSION

Young Oberleutnant Frömsdorf was placed in command of the U-boat's crew of veterans and a few new men. He made a few short training missions to orient the new crewmembers. Then, on February 24, 1945, *U-853* slipped out of Stavanger, Norway, one of Germany's alternative operational centers, and into the Atlantic, headed for the New England Coast — this time never to return.

On March 19, a routine report was made to headquarters. On April 1, *U-853* was ordered to operate in the Gulf of Maine, concentrating off Boston or, if conditions were unfavorable,

alternative areas were Halifax or New York.

Prowling the southern New England coast, *U-853* is thought to have sunk the submarine-chaser *Eagle 56* with her crew of 49, on April 23. That speculation will never be confirmed because events aboard *U-853* during her final days remain lost with those who died with her. Even though there are no records, it is certain that discomfort, tedium, unwashed bodies, and U-boat duties were part of each day. Phonograph records, books, magazines, photographs of loved ones, cards, chess, and checkers did little to offset the monotony of close confinement under constant threat of destruction and death. Relief was provided each time the U-boat cautiously approached the surface to extend a whip antenna for reception of radio news broadcasts. Crewmen clustered around a radio room early in the war would have been cheered by the reports of German successes. April and May of 1945, however, offered only bleak reports of reversals — disheartening to a U-boat crew.

On April 25, the First White Russian Army and the First Ukrainian Army completed encirclement of Berlin. The death of Adolph Hitler was announced by Hamburg radio on May 1, with Grand Admiral Dönitz appointed his successor as head of state. Germany's naval hero was not to preside in glorious triumph, but to negotiate surrender terms for his nation.

The war in Europe was quickly being brought to a close. Several German armies in Northern Europe were scheduled to surrender on May 5 at 8 A.M., European time. Though Field-Marshal Montgomery had accepted an armistice for German forces in north-west Europe, General Eisenhower declined the armistice until a general capitualtion included the Russian front.

On the night of May 4, Dönitz broadcast the following order:

All U-boats. Attention all U-boats. Cease fire at once. Stop all hostile action against Allied shipping. Dönitz.

There is no record that *U-853* ever acknowledged receipt of that order. Samuel Eliot Morison, U.S. Navy Historian, has suggested that she probably never received word. His view seems to be amply substantiated by the subsequent, aggressive action of the U-boat.

During the afternoon of May 5, *U-853* was cruising at periscope depth east of Block Island, Rhode Island. Frömsdorf differed from his predecessor, the more conservative Sommer; Frömsdorf ordered the U-boat closer to the coast. The January 22, 1961, *New York Sunday News* quotes one of the veteran crewmen who fortun-

Early in the war, German military bands and nurses greeted officers of returning U-boats with flowers. Here, officers from *U-853* are holding welcome home bouquets after return to a French port from a successful weather reconnaissance mission. Such demonstrations died out toward the end of the war. Courtesy of Fred Benson.

ately missed the last mission due to illness. In his comparison of the two captains:

> Frömsdorf was a different personality. At least one crewman aboard believed Frömsdorf was out to get a decoration.

Another crewman, 20-year-old Frederick Volk, had told his mother that he feared the mission because he had no faith in Frömsdorf. Frau Sommer, the wife of Kapitänleutnant Helmut Sommer, stated in a letter in 1974:

> Frömsdorf was very young and ambitious when he became commander after my husband was wounded, and my husband asked him again and again not to act frivolous, for he knew, the end of the war was near and he hoped so much, that all the fine fellows of the crew could survive.

Slowly, "Tightrope Walker" approached Point Judith, a small peninsula that juts out from the Rhode Island shoreline. *U-853* was in the heavily traveled route for ships making the New York to Boston run. She was moving into very dangerous waters. Newport, just 10 miles northeast of Point Judith, was the largest destroyer base on the northeast coast.

Scanning the seas by periscope, Frömsdorf sighted two freighters, a tanker, a tug hauling three barges and the small collier SS *Black Point*, a 5,353-ton, 27-year-old coal carrier which probably would have been scrapped if the war hadn't forced to sea practically everything that could float. Yet, that unattractive relic was to serve as the marauding U-boat's victim. A more likely target would have been the loaded tanker. Why then, *Black Point*? Captain Alexander W. Moffat, USNR (Ret) offers his explanation in *A Navy Maverick Comes of Age, 1939-1945*:

> The target, a new heavily laden oil tanker bound for New York via Long Island Sound passed a coal laden steamer *Black Point* proceeding on opposite course. Boston bound. The turbine driven tanker was relatively silent. The submarine which lay in wait fired a new type of torpedo designed to be guided sonically to target. However, the collier, an old clunker driven by a reciprocating steam engine, passed too close to the torpedo which obediently changed course to the loud noise.

Black Point was entering the western end of Rhode Island Sound, four miles southeast of Point Judith at 5:40 P.M. Without warning, a torpedo explosion tore away 40 feet of her stern. The acoustic type torpedo was designed to home on the sounds of ships' screws, and struck aft where the engines and steering apparatus were located. Several crewmen were killed immediately. Others were to die in the following minutes. *Black Point* was sinking fast by what was left of her stern. At 5:55 P.M., the collier rolled to her portside, capsized, and sank within sight of land. Twelve of the crew went to the bottom with her. The surviving crewmen and the Navy gun crew escaped in life rafts. A total of 34 men, including two injured, were eventually rescued.

The 368-foot, steel hulled *Black Point*, built in 1918 at Camden, N.J., now lies 3¾ miles southeast of Point Judith Lighthouse, in 85 feet of water. She was the last U-boat victim off the American coast, but the last success by a German U-boat in the Second World War occurred a day later. *U-2336* (Klusmeyer) sank the freighters *Avondale Park* (2,878 tons) and *Sneland* (1,791 tons) off the Firth of Forth in the North Sea on May 7.

The crew of a nearby Yugoslav freighter, *Kamen*, witnessed *Black Point's* explosion and two minutes later sent out an SOS and warning of a U-boat in the area. Although only 10 miles away, the Newport Naval Base could not help. That day, Newport could send out nothing formidable enough to hunt and kill a U-boat.

FOX AND HOUNDS

"Tightrope Walker's" luck seemed to be holding, but in fact it had just run out. Unfortunately for *U-853*, part of U.S. Navy Task Force 60.7 was only 30 miles off in the vicinity of the Cape Cod Canal, en route to the Boston Navy Yard for repairs and provisions. The escort group had just returned with GUS-84, a convoy from Gibraltar, delivering merchant ships to Norfolk, Philadelphia, and New York City.

The Yugoslav freighter's SOS was received by the Coast Guard frigate *Moberly,* and was relayed to two U.S. Navy destroyer escorts, *Amick* and *Atherton*. Lieutenant Commander L.B. Tollaksen, USCG, commanding officer of the frigate was the senior officer of the three vessels. He directed *Atherton* to the scene of the sinking and to sweep south from that position. *Amick* was to search Block Island Sound westward of the sinking, while *Moberly* was assigned the eastern approaches. All three ships were to maintain extreme sonar alert en route to their assigned areas.

A fourth warship, the destroyer *Ericsson* was far ahead having already entered the Cape Cod Canal. Aboard *Ericsson* was the convoy commander, Commander F.C.B. McCune, USN. Tollaksen attempted to communicate with McCune, but without success. When contact was established shortly before 7 P.M., Tollaksen was designated Officer in Tactical Command until *Ericsson* could reach the scene. *Atherton*, which had just entered Buzzards Bay, steamed at full speed for Point Judith, trailed by *Moberly* and

Black Point, the last ship sunk by U-boat action in American waters during the Second World War, was a victim of *U-853*. The antiquated collier sank with the loss of 12 lives and 7,000 tons of coal. *Black Point* carried a five-inch gun aft manned by four U.S. Navy gunners. One of the gunners was killed when 40 feet of the collier's stern was blown off by *U-853*'s torpedo. Courtesy of National Archives.

Executive Officer Frömsdorf was given command of *U-853* after Captain Sommer was wounded by Allied aircraft. Frömsdorf was in command when the U-boat was lost with all hands. Photo courtesy of David Arnold.

Amick.

As dusk fell, *U-853* was resting quietly on the sandy bottom. She had been in tight spots before and had always eluded her hunters. But this time, she had ventured into shallow coastal waters with enemy warships bearing down on her.

In deeper water, the U-boat would have had a chance to escape but a submarine cornered in shallow water has little chance because sonar can pinpoint her location more readily and she is an easier target for depth charges. Frau Sommer stated in a letter that her husband Kapitänleutnant Helmut Sommer:

> . . . often and often told me, that he never had attacked a ship in such a situation, *U-853* was lost from the beginning with such little water under the keel and so near the coast . . . I remembered all the fine young men in the crew I knew so very well. They were convinced to fight for a good matter ready to do their duty and misguided by a devil. I can only pray, that such a madness never will come again.

There is evidence, however, that Frömsdorf was following orders. Dönitz in *Memoirs: Ten Years and Twenty Days* wrote that during the last year of the war:

> It was repeatedly stressed to commanders that they should always act in a manner which would be unexpected by the enemy; for example when attacking . . . attack from shallow waters . . . they should similarly try to escape inshore.

By 7:30 P.M., the three American ships reached the scene and prepared for the prearranged sweep of the area. *Atherton,* because of her excellent sonar team, was assigned to what Tollaksen determined was the most likely escape route of the U-boat. At 8:14 P.M., *Atherton* picked up a sonar contact. The returning echo was so unusual and unfamiliar that *Atherton* was convinced that this contact was the enemy submarine. It was; *U-853* had been located less than three hours after the sinking of *Black Point.*

The two other ships stopped their own sonar search and listened to *Atherton*'s echo ranging, while the sonar operators of the three ships discussed the characteristics of the signal by radio. It was determined that the contact was moving slowly along a course of 90 degrees true. When the operators were satisfied that they could recognize the unfamiliar echo, *Atherton* began her attack. At 8:29 P.M., she dropped 13 depth charges set on magnetic. The center one exploded, indicating it had struck metal.

Several minutes later *Atherton* made a second run, using Hedgehogs. An attacking ship passes over a U-boat to drop conventional depth charges — an action that breaks sonar contact. The Hedgehog is a mortar designed to fire a pattern of 24 charges ahead of instead of behind the attacking ship, to explode on actual contact with the U-boat's hull. A second Hedgehog attack resulted in many smaller explosions, but it was uncertain whether any hit the U-boat or had exploded on the hard bottom. By then, the water was so agitated that *Atherton* lost sonar contact.

The U.S. warships were still wary of the U-boat. *Amick* was withdrawn from the attacking group with orders to join *Booth,* another destroyer escort from Task Group 60.7, as escort for a merchant ship from New York to Boston via Cape Cod. *Ericsson* was still an hour away. Thus, it was left to *Atherton* and *Moberly* to destroy the U-boat.

There was some uncertainty as to whether *Atherton* had been attacking a submarine or some old wreckage. It was decided to break off the attack and expand the search area for the U-boat in case she had slipped by the group. Before leaving the position of her three attacks, *Atherton* dropped a lighted buoy for future reference. *Ericsson* and seven other destroyers arrived, and Commander McCune took over as Officer in Tactical Command. A picket line was formed to keep the apparently damaged U-boat from escaping to deeper water.

When contact had not been reestablished by 10 P.M., *Moberly* and *Atherton* moved several miles away and worked their way back toward the last known position of the U-boat. *Atherton* soon picked up a radar contact, thought to be the schnorchel of the German submarine. Searchlights revealed that it was only a small unlighted buoy. "Tightrope Walker" had slipped out of the area but *Atherton* resumed search and picked her up at 11:23 P.M. The U-boat was sitting on the bottom at a depth of 100 feet, 4,000 yards east of the original attack area. Sonar contact was lost at 11:33 P.M. and found again four minutes later. Ten minutes later, still in sonar contact, another pattern of Hedgehogs was fired. Bubbles of air and oil erupted from the sea followed by pieces of wood, a life jacket, a mattress, and bits of cork, all suggesting that the U-boat might have been hit, but with no assurance. *U-853* had an experienced crew, familiar with such old U-boat tricks as firing debris through torpedo tubes to convince their pursuers they had been destroyed.

When *Atherton* picked up the debris with her searchlights, May 6 was 31 minutes old. *Atherton* circled the area for about 20 minutes, maintaining sonar contact. There was no noticeable movement of the U-boat and no noise from her crew. Commander McCune ordered *Atherton* to cross

U-853's sinking was officially credited to the U.S.N. destroyer escort *Atherton (DE-169)* and the U.S.C.G. frigate *Moberly (PF-63)*. *Atherton* was awarded one battle star for her successful encounter with the U-boat. A. Hedgehog. B. Depth charges. Courtesy of National Archives.

over the spot with her fathometer in order to determine the exact position of the U-boat, and then follow with another attack. *Atherton* bore in with what was thought to be the *coup de grace:* a barrage of 13 depth charges, set to explode at a depth of 75 feet. The shallow setting was used for fear that if set for 100 feet (the actual depth of the U-boat) the charges might land on the bottom before exploding. Again, oil, air bubbles, a pillow, a small wood flagstaff, and another life jacket appeared. *Moberly* and *Atherton* scanned the area with searchlights for other wreckage that might have surfaced.

Shortly after 1 A.M. *Atherton* was ordered to resume attack, and another 13 depth charges were dropped directly over the U-boat. One exploded too close to the destroyer escort, jarring loose some of her sonar gear. The shallow setting of the charges had not allowed enough time for the destroyer to clear the area.

As *Moberly* moved in to take *Atherton*'s place, she discovered the U-boat, incredibly, still very much alive. "Tightrope Walker" was creeping along near the bottom, at a speed of 4 or 5 knots. *Moberly* fired a salvo of depth charges, but to

reduce the danger of damage such as *Atherton* had just received from the shallow-exploding depth charges, she increased her attack speed to 18 knots, higher than general practice. Even with that change in tactics, depth charges damaged her steering mechanism. As she bore down for a second Hedgehog run, mechanical problems forced her to abort the attack. All action was suspended while the U.S. warships stood off to make repairs.

By 2 A.M. *Moberly*'s repairs were completed and she began another attack, using hedgehogs to avoid damaging herself. Because of the earlier pounding the frigate had taken, her firing panel was damaged and the attack was broken off. It was noted that the submarine was now moving about two or three knots at 75 feet. Then *Moberly* lost contact.

Commander McCune ordered the other destroyers to assist and assigned them to specific search areas. Because of her excellent sonar crew, *Atherton* was assigned the area of last contact. *Atherton* regained contact, but no further attacks were made that night.

At dawn, an oil slick over a mile wide covered

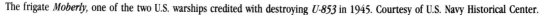

The frigate *Moberly,* one of the two U.S. warships credited with destroying *U-853* in 1945. Courtesy of U.S. Navy Historical Center.

Underwater explosions from a pattern of detonating Hedgehogs cause the water to boil in front of *Moberly. Atherton* can be seen on the horizon awaiting her turn to attack *U-853*. Courtesy of National Archives.

USS *Ericsson (DD-440)* joined the hunt for *U-853* one and a half hours after the attack began. Commander F.C.B. McCune, USN, aboard the destroyer became Officer in Tactical Command. More than 12 hours later McCune declared *U-853* sunk. Courtesy of U.S. Naval Historical Center.

the surface. Three pools of oil, spaced 30 feet apart were reported to be coming from the U-boat. Floating throughout it were German escape lungs, life jackets, several life rafts, abandon-ship kits complete with canteens and emergency rations, deck planking, the top of a chart table with the designation *U-853,* and an officer's cap.

McCune ordered the attack continued at 5:30 that morning. The three ships, including *Ericsson,* combined Hedgehog and depth charge attacks in an attempt to crack the U-boat's pressure hull. One of the ships would attack, then drift off to make repairs while a second ship in the circle would move in to attack. By the time the third ship had finished her attack, the first ship was ready to re-start the cycle. Damage suffered by the attackers was less than before because in addition to increasing speed by several knots, they also increased the depth settings on the charges.

A sailor in a whaleboat retrieves wreckage from the oil slick after *U-853* was sunk by U.S. warships. Courtesy of National Archives.

A gold braided officer's cap in the midst of debris recovered from *U-853*. The cap was awarded to Lt. Commander Lewis Islin, captain of the destroyer escort *Atherton* because the sinking was credited to the vessel's outstanding sonar detection. Courtesy of National Archives.

Two Navy ZNP type dirigibles, *K-16* and *K-58* from Lakehurst, New Jersey, appeared over the scene about 6:00 and *K-16* dropped a sonobuoy, a sonar device used frequently by Hunter-Killer groups. Floating on the surface, it transmitted underwater sounds to aircraft. *K-16* reported to McCune that she had strong contact and the target was "stationary." McCune then ordered four more attacks on the U-boat.

The sonobuoy picked up a kind of voiceless farewell, which was received by the sonar operators in both blimps. They described it as a, rhythmic hammering on a metal surface which was interrupted periodically.

K-16 attacked with rockets, one of which landed squarely in the middle of the three aligned geysers of air and oil. Again, planks of wood and an abandon-ship kit broke the surface.

The second blimp moved into position and fired more rockets. Then it was the turn of the warships to attack. First, *Atherton*, with a barrage of depth charges, followed by *Moberly* with Hedgehogs. Then *Atherton* fired a salvo of Hedgehogs, followed by *Moberly*, to make the last run.

Moberly's Commander reported a very large eruption of air and oil was followed by canteens, papers, life raft, and miscellaneous debris. The battle ended at 10:45 A.M. when Commander McCune declared ". . . the submarine was sunk and on the bottom . . ."

The warships had launched a tremendous number of depth charges and Hedgehogs. The monstrous detonations would have pounded against the U-boat with sledgehammer blows. The crew was probably thrown about inside like toys until concussions finally blew the pressure hull open and the sea rushed in. There were no survivors. *U-853* is today the underwater tomb for all but two of her crew, most in their 20's, a few 19 year-olds, and one 18. Frömsdorf had just turned 24.

It surprised Commander McCune and others on the scene that the U-boat made no attempt to surface or fire her torpedoes. She was probably critically damaged early. Otherwise, Frömsdorf would have blown the ballast tanks and surfaced to give his crew at least a chance to escape before she sank.

The destroyers grappled for the submarine with anchors, one of which remains today, lying in the sand with its chain still draped over the conning tower of *U-853*.

Practice Hedgehog runs continued until 12:24

P.M., when one of the destroyers marked the sunken U-boat with a buoy line. Then McCune ordered his ships to proceed to Boston and detached the others.

"Tightrope Walker" had fallen from her high wire with no net; *U-853* was officially dead. Nine hours and 17 minutes after the last Hedgehogs were dropped on *U-853,* German Chief-of-Staff General Alfred Jodl and Admiral Georg Friedeburg, Dönitz' friend and personal representative, signed unconditional surrender papers at Reims, France. It was 2:41 A.M. May 7 in France, and 9:41 P.M. May 6 over the grave of *U-853.* Formal surrender terms were concluded at Berlin the next day, with the terms becoming effective at 12:01 A.M. (European time) on May 9.

Two of these men perished with *U-853*, radio operator Erich Schoadt (center) and machinist petty officer Helmut Fehrs (at left). W. Dechen, at right, was transferred from *U-853* before her last cruise. Courtesy of Fred Benson.

Surrender of Germany at Reims, France, right to left, Admiral Hans-Georg Friedeburg, Commander-in-Chief of the German Navy, Colonel General Alfred Jodl, Chief of Staff of the German Army, and Major Wilhelm Oxenius. Courtesy of National Archives.

U-853 was the last U-boat sunk in American waters, but not the last of the war. An RAF Catalina flying boat (210 Squadron) sank *U-320* off Bergen on May 7.

Atherton, because of the outstanding performance of her sonar crew, was credited with the kill of *U-853,* with *Moberly* assisting. Lieutenant Commander Lewis Iselin, USNR, commanding officer of *Atherton,* was awarded the Legion of Merit. Lieutenant Commander L.B. Tollaksen, USCG, commanding officer of *Moberly,* was awarded the Bronze Star with Combat "V" for setting up the search patterns that initially located *U-853.*

On the afternoon of May 6, Navy divers from the salvage ship *Penguin* followed the buoy line to the battered U-boat at the request of Naval Intelligence. The divers were ordered to penetrate the U-boat and recover papers from the Captain's safe but they failed. The bulky suits of surface-tended divers make such penetration difficult.

The next day, Edwin J.R. Bockelman volunteered to try again. He was the smallest diver aboard the salvage ship and felt that he could squeeze through the conning tower hatch. Commander George W. Albin, Jr., skipper of *Penguin,* accepted Bockelman's offer on condition that he accompany him. Albin wanted to be close by if Bockelman became trapped inside the U-boat.

They dove together to the conning tower, and Albin waited while Bockelman squeezed through the open hatch. Inside, the bodies of six crewmen blocked his path. The macabre sentries barred further entry. He struggled out through the hatch, using his feet to pull one of the bodies out with him. Albin aided Bockelman and together they managed to extract the body through the hatch. The corpse, bearing the identification tag, H. Hoffman UO 28177-41S, had been a husky, good looking, 22-year-old seaman. Navy divers made only one other dive on the U-boat, but nothing was recovered. They reported at least 12 unexploded depth charges and the Navy decided not to take any more chances. Bockelman received the Navy and Marine Corps Medal for his feat.

MYSTERY CARGO

U-853 lies on the bottom of the Atlantic, 130 feet down, 7 miles east of Block Island, R.I. Before Frömsdorf left on his last voyage, he told his mother he was going on a vital mission from which he would not return. *U-853,* he told her, carried a great secret. One of his subordinates, Engineering Officer Christian Wilde, confided to a friend before departing on his last mission that there was something aboard the U-boat that he

could not talk about. Eight years passed before anyone visited *U-853* in an effort to unlock her secret, if indeed she possessed one.

In September 1953, at Newport, Rhode Island: a stranger approached the captain of the 50-foot fishing boat *Maureen* with an offer to hire the boat and captain at the rate of $200 a day. The boat's captain, Gilbert Brownell, asked why he wanted the charter, and Oswald L. Bonifay replied that he wanted to look for submarines. Brownell agreed to the deal.

The next day Bonifay returned with a list of several German U-boats sunk near the U.S. coast during the war. He pointed to *U-853* and said that she was the one he was principally interested in. Then he showed Brownell blueprints of the U-boat and several German documents which pertained to her. Bonifay said he had obtained the location and plans of *U-853* through contacts in the U.S. Navy. He offered no explanation of why he was seeking the U-boats. Bonifay had an aura of mystery about him all the while.

New scuba diving equipment from southern France was loaded aboard the fishing boat. Bonifay casually remarked that he had been in France shortly before and had ordered the equipment shipped directly to Newport. Next, two professional hard-hat divers from Boston, Bill Mercer and William George, appeared. Their high salaries, like Brownell's, were always paid in cash. Bonifay paid cash for everything and was remembered as the biggest tipper the local hotel (Cliff Walk Manor) had ever had.

With the aid of what Brownell described as hundreds of charts and diagrams, *U-853* was located on the second day out. Bonifay made every trip to the wreck site, and from 6 A.M. to 10 P.M., he prowled the deck of the fishing boat or pored over his documents, all in German. The divers were ordered to report directly and confidentially to Bonifay as soon as they surfaced.

Bonifay was as interested in *U-853*'s captains quarters, as Naval Intelligence had been. Once, when he needed more detailed plans Bonifay radioed Bremerhaven. A few days later, he had the plans.

Seventeen times, Bonifay dove to *U-853,* using an aqualung. He said nothing of his findings and he instructed all concerned with the operation to refrain from discussing it. He barred everyone from the fishing boat except those concerned with the project.

Brownell considered Bonifay the most mysterious man he had ever met, but he had a lot of money and, to the fisherman, that was what counted.

Even with all the secrecy surrounding the

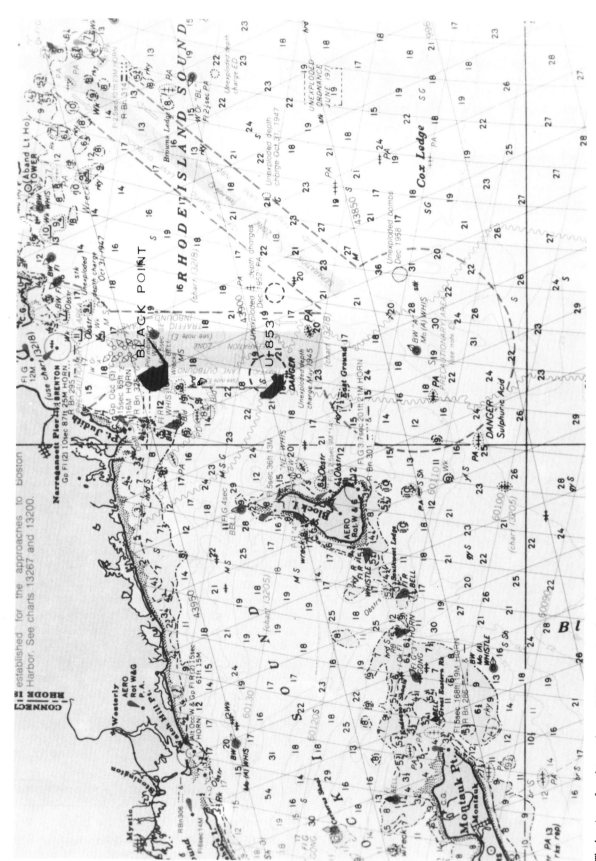

The locations of predator and prey. *U-853* rests only a few miles south of *Black Point*. This illustration should not be used for navigational purposes.

The U.S. Navy used an anchor to grapple for *U-853* after sinking her. The anchor chain is still draped around the U-boat's conning tower with the anchor in the sand beside her. Photo by Mike Casalino.

mission, rumors circulated around the Newport waterfront that Bonifay was after a fabulous treasure: gold bullion or flasks of mercury. It was even rumored that *U-853* was to have been Hitler's getaway boat, en route to South America. One rumor that has made the rounds is that *U-853* had on board from $500,000 to $1,000,000 in jewels and U.S. currency, smuggled on board by her Captain in sealed 37mm shell cases. The valuables were reportedly part of the loot taken from the American Express vaults when the Germans captured France. The money, wrapped in waterproof paper, was said to have been welded in nine shell cases. Five other cases were reported to have contained jewels. This possibility is supported by testimony at the Nuremberg War Crime Trials that traveler's checks were welded in *U-853* shell cases, as reported in the November 7, 1969 issue of the *Westerly Sun*, a Rhode Island newspaper. It has been speculated that the shell cases were to be hidden on U.S. soil and recovered later. Frau Sommer reported in a letter that she and Kapitänleutnant Sommer had heard rumors about treasure on board *U-853:*

> ... but a former member of the crew, responsible for the equipment, and who became fortunately for himself sick one day before *U-853* left Stavanger told us, that there was nothing unusual about *U-853* and that all the rumors were absolutely nonsense.

Unaffected by all the speculation, the divers continued their search during the raw, New England fall days. Unexploded depth charges were still in view. Fog frequently shrouded the boat, concealing her from the view of large passing ships as they plied the steamer lane close by. Curious sharks occasionally prowled the vicinity.

Professional diver William George, making as many as four dives a day, twice suffered attacks of the bends, a potentially fatal condition caused by the buildup of nitrogen in a diver's body. Bonifay's divers did remove the two bronze propellers from *U-853* but there is no indication that he recovered what he was seeking.

Eight years later, in 1961, the mysterious Bonifay broke his silence about the U-boat's secret. He declared that he was after more than $1,000,000 worth of mercury secreted somewhere in the U-boat. Bonifay said the mercury was still in the U-boat, and that he could not get it out.

Bonifay claimed the mercury was contained in stainless steel flasks and was being dispatched to Japan, to be traded for tin. He had no explanation for *U-853*'s presence off the New England coast. But it is true that U-boats were dispatched from Germany to Japan carrying mercury, optical instruments, radar sets and dismantled V-weapons. Those that survived the round trip returned to Germany with cargoes of zinc, tin, raw rubber, quinine, and opium. Torpedoes were only carried for emergency use. Their normal storage places were reserved for cargo.

In September, 1944, a Type IXD$_2$, U-boat, *U-859,* bound for Malaysia and Singapore, was sunk in the shallows of Malacca Straits. The U-boat's cargo of 30 tons of mercury, salvaged in 1972, was valued at $17.7 million. The Federal German Republic's claim that the vessel and its cargo were the property of the Bonn government was upheld in the courts.

In 1961, Bonifay dismissed the *U-853* venture as a vacation project; he failed to mention that the operation lasted 10 weeks and cost him at least $20,000. However, he did acknowledge that he had returned to Newport a few years later for another try. On that occasion, he was so secretive that Brownell didn't even know that he had returned.

William George, the diver who had twice suffered the bends trying to unravel *U-853*'s secret, also returned. It wasn't known whether he was free lancing or employed by Bonifay. George, then 51, made his last known dive to the U-boat on May 8, 1959, and again suffered the bends. He was rushed to a Navy recompression chamber where it took 63 hours to rid his body of the

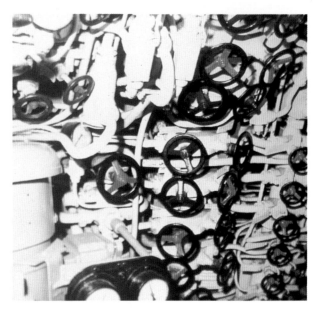

Inside *U-505*'s control room. Photo by Jerry Lawrence.

The same controls in *U-853*. Photo by Bill Campbell.

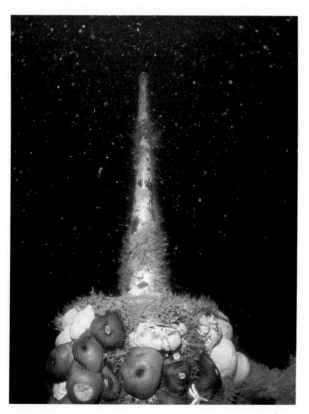

Divers sawed off the upper portion of the attack periscope. Photo by Bill Campbell.

trapped nitrogen. George informed Navy personnel that he had been seeking mercury.

Except for occasional scuba divers who dove to the submarine and picked up souvenirs, no serious attempt to solve the mystery of the U-boat was made until 1960.

SKELETAL REMAINS

Burton H. Mason of Trumbull, Ct. and four other Connecticut scuba divers joined in an extensive research project to find out all that could be learned about *U-853*. In May, 1960, they dove down to have their first look at her. By coincidence it was May 6, the 15th anniversary of the U-boat's destruction.

Mason became obsessed with *U-853*. He quit his job as a heating engineer, and left his home in Trumbull to live as close as possible to the U-boat. He spent all his savings, then he begged and borrowed financial backing.

Mason penetrated the U-boat on a later dive but his powerful underwater light scarcely cut through the disturbed sediment. The light etched sudden, unforgettable images: skeletons scattered throughout the U-boat, escape gear draped about them, charts, books with the paper still good in them, binoculars, and sextants laying around as though they had just been set down by someone.

Mason and his friends brought up six life rafts, sawed off the upper eight inches of one of the periscopes for a souvenir, and removed a number of human bones. In June, 1960, Mason brought up a skeleton from the conning tower. Although the probability of treasure aboard the U-boat was an undeniable spur, Mason wanted to learn more about the lives and deaths of the men aboard her. He wanted to bring up the dead of *U-853* for proper burial, but the West German government was cool to the proposal. While Mason argued with German officials, the remains of the unknown *U-853* crewman lay in a Newport funeral home. The Germans claimed Mason had desecrated their war dead and warned him not to bring up any more skeletons or attempt to raise the U-boat. Mason charged that Germany had reneged on a previous agreement giving him salvage rights. He claimed that Hitler's Third Reich, not the Federal Republic of West Germany, legally owned *U-853*.

The German consul in Boston, Gerhard Lang, was the official with whom Mason was feuding. The February 5, 1961, New York *Sunday News* quotes Lang's denial that *U-853* carried a "treasure:"

> Only the normal amounts of mercury maintained for the operation of any submarine, and no surplus amounts, were on the vessel, according to an investigation made into official war records by the German government . . . . the German government looks on this plan of Mason's as a commercial venture aimed at exploiting the dead, and no civilized society approves of this.

The Germans were not the only ones opposed to Mason's plan. Two retired U.S. Navy admirals living in Newport publicly denounced him. Nine Newport clergymen petitioned the U.S. government to prevent him from disturbing the dead.

Open deck hatches invite a curious diver, John Lachenmeyer, to penetrate *U-853*'s interior compartments, often a tight fit. Photo by H. Keatts.

Meanwhile a West German magazine, *New Illustrated,* reported the story of Mason's activities and received an interesting response. One man, Theodore Womer, a member of *U-853*'s crew from the time of her commissioning, appeared with a death certificate showing he had died in the U-boat. He had missed the fateful last mission due to illness.

It took the West German government four months to decide what to do with the skeleton Mason had retrieved. In October, 1960, the *U-853* crewman was buried in a rain swept cemetery in Newport, R.I., with full U.S. military honors. A chaplain from the Newport Naval Station officiated at the burial of the anonymous seaman while West German representatives looked on.

In 1968 the Murphy Pacific Marine Salvage Co. of New York and Emeryville, California received a contract to raise *U-853*. Melvin L. Joseph Recovery Corporation of Georgetown, Delaware, reportedly wanted the U-boat for an exhibit as a tourist attraction. Captain Paul Brasack, at that time naval attache at the German embassy in Washington, said Melvin Joseph was granted permission to do as he pleased with the wreck but the remains of the crew and their personal effects were to be turned over to the West German government for disposal. Captain Brasack also said *U-853* was on a normal, offensive mission when she was sunk and he doubted that the U-boat contained anything in the way of treasure. Murphy Pacific was unsuccessful. The following year the Joseph Recovery Corporation contracted Ventures Inter-

U-505, the only surviving Type IXC U-boat in the world was the first enemy ship captured by the U.S. Navy on the high seas since 1815. The U-boat is shown in place on the east side of the Chicago Museum of Science and Industry. A crowd of 15,000 witnessed the formal dedication of the U-boat as a memorial to the 55,000 Americans who perished at sea in two world wars. Courtesy of Chicago Museum of Science and Industry.

U-853 RESTING ON THE BOTTOM

1. Propellers were removed by divers
2. Opening into aft torpedo room, about 15 feet in diameter
3. Deck gun's barrel and flak shield were accidentally torn off in 1981
4. Circular hatch
5. Navy anchor in the sand, with the chain draped over the conning tower
6. Opening in the outer hull, but not the pressure hull
7. Periscopes were sawed off by divers
8. Conning tower hatch
9. An opening, four feet in diameter, into the commander's quarters and radio room allows easy access to the control room
10. Circular hatch to officer's quarters
11. Square hatch into crew's quarters
12. Forward torpedo room hatch
13. Air canister
14. Opening in outer hull, exposing torpedo tube

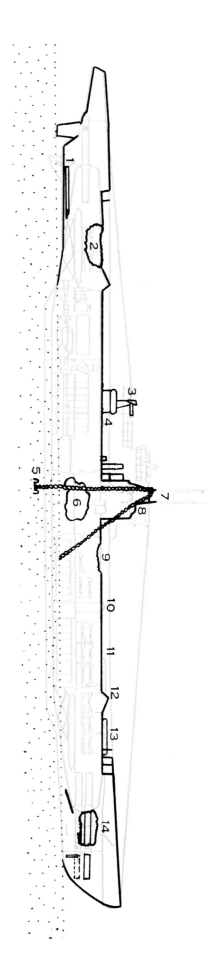

139

national Incorporated of Harvey, Louisiana for another attempt.

Nothing came of the salvage efforts and *U-853* still rests in her sandy grave. However, salvage attempts have continued, as recently as 1981. Those efforts have undoubtedly been stimulated by the many stories of *U-853*'s mission and cargo that persist even today.

SPORT DIVING

U-853 is now a popular dive spot, regularly visited by sport divers. The U-boat lies seven miles due east of Block Island in 127 feet of water, sitting upright on the sandy bottom. Her cryptic monument, a circle labeled "Danger, unexploded depth charges," can be seen on the navigational chart of the choppy, tide-ripped waters of Rhode Island Sound.

The pressure hull was originally enclosed by a thin steel envelope, designed to streamline the U-boat. The corrosive effects of years under the sea have removed most of the outer covering. The wooden decking is gone, exposing a mass of tangled gridwork and pipes. The conning tower does not look as one might expect, because the flak shield corroded away long ago, and the upper part of the periscopes were cut off. Only the conning tower's pressure hull and periscope stalks remain.

The cranium of a skull inside *U-853*. Photo by H. Keatts.

A skull and other skeletal remains inside *U-853*'s victim, *Black Point*. Twelve of the collier's crew went to the bottom with her. Photo by Bill Campbell.

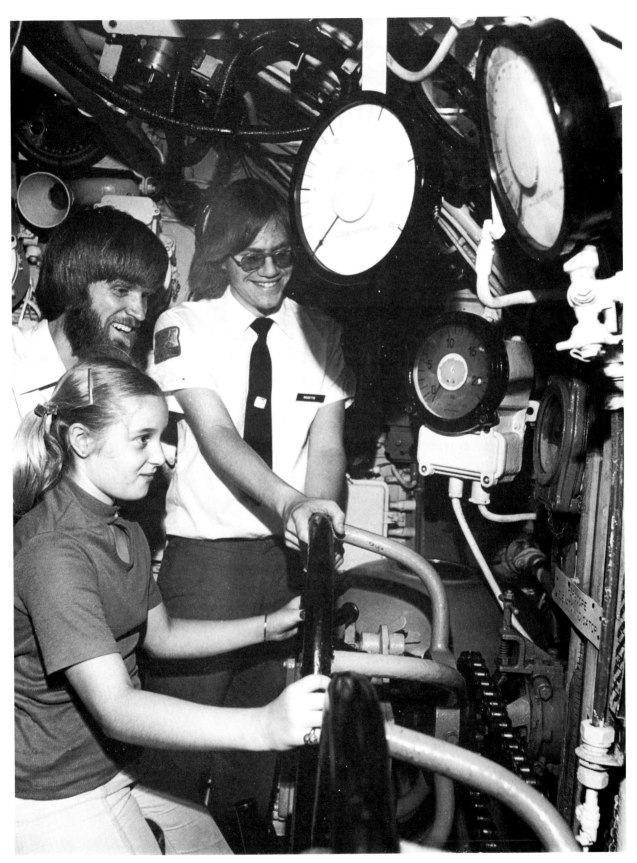

U-505 is open to the public. This compartment, located amidships, is the U-boat's nerve center and contains the important diving and steering controls. A visitor turns one of the two hydroplane controls in the control room. Courtesy of *Chicago Museum of Science and Industry.*

Hydroplane controls as they appear today within *U-853*'s control room. Photo by Bill Campbell.

A bicycle-type seat (on left) and the base of the sky periscope (upper left) within the control room. Photo by H. Keatts.

U-853's control room with 20mm ammunition stacked to be passed through the conning tower to the anti-aircraft machine guns on the "winter garden," the small deck behind the conning tower. Photo by H. Keatts.

H. Keatts passing through hatch leading from control room into radio room. For maximum strength the interior hatchways were circular. Photo by Steve Bielenda.

Ammunition for *U-853*'s 20mm anti-aircraft guns. The powder bag has the date October 1944. Due to the scarcity of brass the shell casings were made of steel. Photo by H. Keatts.

Steve Bielenda, captain and owner of the dive charter boat *Wahoo,* holds a round and clip of 20mm ammunition. Photo by H. Keatts.

Abandon-ship kit recovered by Henry Keatts in 1985 contained cigarettes (with paper disintegrated, but tobacco intact), provisions, sunburn ointment, and one-man raft that inflated after 40 years underwater. Photos by Steve Bielenda.

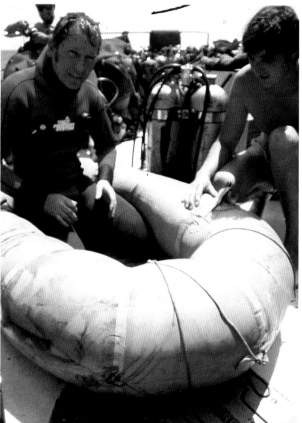

One-man life raft recovered in 1945 after the destruction of *U-853*. Courtesy of National Archives.

The authors, George Farr (left) holding the bailing cup and Henry Keatts holding the sea anchor, with the one-man raft recovered in 1985. Photo by Carole Keatts.

A maze of dials, valves, and gauges cover the interior hull of *U-505*'s conning tower. The attack periscope and seat are at right; torpedo data computer at left; pre-set firing controls, center. Courtesy of Chicago Museum of Science and Industry.

Inside *U-853*'s conning tower — note ladder and hatch with cover between conning tower and the control room below. Photo by Bill Campbell.

Several open deck hatches invite the curious to penetrate *U-853*'s interior compartments. The conning tower hatch has been removed and a diver can enter easily with a single tank. Because of the extensive damage caused by the Navy's furious attack, there are several other places for divers to enter the hull. Forward of the conning tower, the pressure hull is blown open and a diver with a set of double air tanks can easily enter through the gaping hole. From that point, the diver can pass through a circular hatch and enter the control room, which appeared quite different in 1945 than it does today. The compartment contained most of the principal controls for operating the U-boat but massive deterioration has occurred and divers have removed most of the gauges and instruments.

U-505 gauge above the engine room hatch. Photo by Tom Roach.

The same gauge in *U-853* after three decades underwater (when the photo was taken). Photo by Tom Roach.

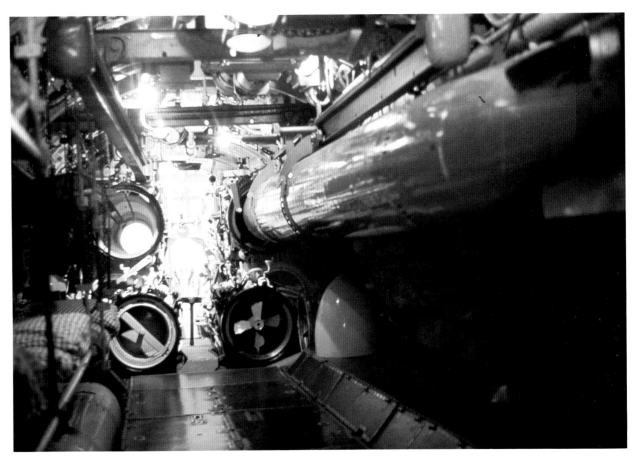

Forward torpedo room of *U-505* contains four torpedo tubes. Most of the crew shared quarters here. A torpedo is suspended from the chain hoist used during loading. Another is shown in its storage space with the deck plates removed. Each torpedo fired at an enemy ship increased the crew's living space. Photo courtesy of Tom Roach.

Forward torpedo room of *U-853*, showing torpedo tube door decorated with a woman's name, Hannelore. The C clamp was installed during a salvage attempt in 1968. A deflated weather balloon can be seen below the door. Photo by H. Keatts.

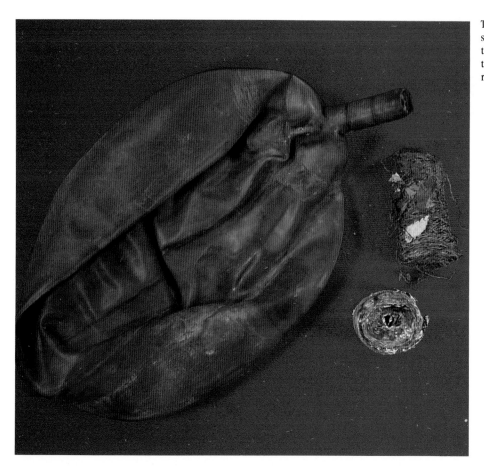

The balloon, still inflatable, is shown with a roll of string and tin foil that was suspended under the balloon to confuse enemy radar. Photo by H. Keatts.

Tail of torpedo in *U-853*'s forward torpedo room, showing fins and propeller. Photo by H. Keatts.

Nine millimeter pistol and ammunition recovered from *U-853* by Larry Keen. Photo by H. Keatts.

Assorted tags removed from *U-853* by Larry Keen. Photo by H. Keatts.

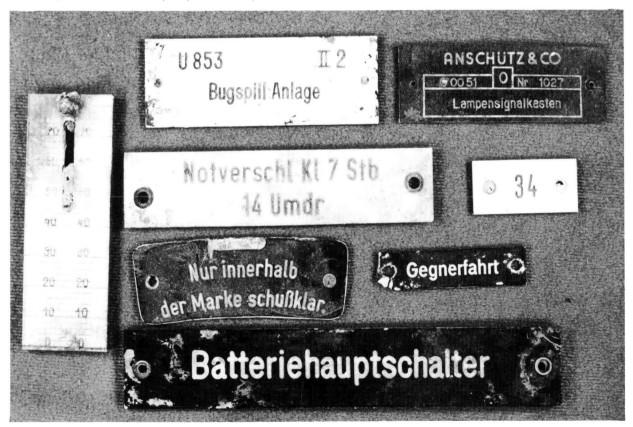

Carole Keatts swims past the 37mm anti-aircraft gun on the U-boat's stern. In 1981 the barrel and flak shield were accidentally torn off by a salvage boat's mooring line. Photo by Mike Casalino.

The 37mm anti-aircraft gun on the U-boat's stern, designed to fire 100 shells a minute, was a photographer's delight until the gun barrel and flak shield were accidentally torn off by a salvage boat's mooring line. The two 20mm anti-aircraft guns were removed by divers.

The Navy anchor that had grappled for the U-boat still lies in the sand amongst wreckage on the starboard side, even with the conning tower. The anchor chain remains draped over the conning tower.

It is a thoughtful experience to dive the deeper *U-853* and follow with a dive on her victim, *Black Point,* the last ship to be torpedoed off the coast of the United States in World War II. The common grave of predator and prey symbolizes the futility of mankind's inhumanity to his own in a cause that succeeds or is thwarted only until history repeats itself in yet another confrontation.

CHAPTER NINE

SUPER SUB-TOO LATE — U-2513

Admiral Karl Dönitz, Uncle Karl to Nazi Germany's adulating submariners, sat in somber conference with Adolph Hitler to revamp the naval strategy of World War II. It was 1942, a year that had opened with Germany's U-boats enjoying the "Happy Time," and Germany was close to controlling the major sea lanes of the Atlantic. Over seven and a half million tons of Allied shipping had already been sunk, accounting for 1,570 Allied ships. Winston Churchill's "Battle of the Atlantic" was indeed running in Germany's favor as the year opened. There were losses of course. Not all U-boats returned from patrol, but the favorable ratio of 40 Allied ships sunk to one U-boat loss in the first quarter of 1942 was a promising prospect for the rest of the year.

THE TIDE TURNS

Then, airborne radar and powerful searchlights denied U-boats the sanctuary of night to ventilate and recharge batteries. Deadly, half-ton "Killer" depth charges and "Hedgehog" saturation of an area with a rocket-launched pattern of 24 contact-triggered charges increased U-boat vulnerability and losses. Allied Hunter-Killer task forces roamed the Atlantic in a constant search for U-boats. Such groups normally consisted of four escort destroyers and a Jeep Aircraft Carrier converted from a merchant ship. No more was the U-boat safe from air attack out of range of land-based planes. By the end of the war, aircraft were to account for 47% of all U-boat sinkings.

Germany's leaders were increasingly aware of the Allied U-boat counter-offensive as 1942 progressed and U-boat losses multiplied. But they had no idea that U-boat radio communications were being intercepted. Early in the war, a German Enigma code machine had fallen into British hands and British cryptographers had broken the German code. U-boat locations and activity, weather reports, and orders from head-quarters were regularly digested by Allied Intelligence. With that information, convoys were safely re-routed and U-boats were method-ically hunted down for destruction.

Even before the disastrous reversal of U-boat successes, Admiral Dönitz was aware that his prized U-boat fleet was fast becoming obsolescent. As he sat in conference with the Führer in September 1942, he fully realized that the "Battle of the Atlantic" was lost unless more formidable U-boats could be put to sea — and soon. Dr. Hellmuth Walter, a brilliant German submarine engineer, had already designed a truly underwater vessel, one that could operate submerged for extended periods at high speed and dive deeper than any that had preceded her.

U-BOAT DEVELOPMENT

Before the war, Walter had experimented with a turbine engine fueled by a hydrogen-peroxide concentrate called Perhydrol. The Walter turbine required no air for combustion and released heat for propulsion plus the favorable by-products of water vapor and oxygen. Used independently, the process was termed the "Cold Method." Walter incorporated fuel oil into the combustion for a "Hot Method" that increased output appreciably.

Walter's experimental work had produced a submerged speed of 28 knots on a small U-boat of 80 tons. His results with a Type XVII streamlined hull model, slightly under 300 tons, led to the

U-2513, a Type XXI U-boat, was one of the first true submarines. In tonnage, she was more than double the size of a Type VII. After World War II the U-boat was commissioned into the U.S. Navy. Courtesy of the National Archives.

Type XXVI, the ultimate in German submarine design. The new design was to provide a maximum underwater speed of 24 knots for six continuous hours of submerged operation. The first of the Type XXVI series, targeted for November, 1945 completion, was never produced. Admiral Dönitz' needs could not wait until 1945. In desperation, he proposed an alternative to Hitler — immediate mass production of a larger version of Dr. Walter's experimental Type XVII, the 1600-ton Type XVIII, powered by the Walter turbine. The Führer agreed but almost immediately the priority demands for Perhydrol in rocket missiles and for Luftwaffe aircraft threatened the Walter turbine U-boat program for lack of fuel.

ELECTRIC BOAT EMERGES

It would have been futile for the U-boat service to compete with missiles and the air force for fuel so the Type XVIII project was temporarily abandoned but not before its streamlined hull provided the basis of a new design concept. The pressure hull was structured like an inverted figure 8, with the smaller circle at the bottom for storage of vast amounts of Perhydrol fuel. The Walter turbine was replaced by standard, light-weight diesel engines for surface propulsion and the Perhydrol storage area was stacked with banks of storage batteries for underwater operation. The result was the Type XXI "Elektro-boot" (Electric Boat). The new U-boat was truly a submarine. Those that preceeded her went under-water only for short periods, then surfaced to clear the air and charge batteries. Whenever submerged for evasive action or to carry out an underwater attack, speed was sacrificed for security. Submarine was a misnomer for such vessels that more aptly might have been termed "Diving Boats." But that was not true of the Type XXI, designed to operate almost entirely below the surface, at great depths, and at high speed. As large as Germany's largest attack submarine, the Type IXD, it had a surface speed of 15 knots and an operating range of 15,000 miles. But under-water, in her element, the new U-boat was capable of over 17 knots for up to one hour. Even at schnorchel level, she operated at 12 knots, twice as fast as earlier types. The Type XXI was designed to dive 100 meters deeper than earlier U-boats, well beyond depth charge range, and to remain submerged for two days at normal speed or 11 days at slow speed. The Type IXD, by comparison, was limited to 14 hours submerged.

The Type XXI was well equipped for her long periods of submerged operation. An air purification ventilating system, used for the first time

A close-up of the improved schnorchel head of *U-2513.* Courtesy of National Archives.

since World War I, a food freezer, and a garbage disposal unit all contributed to the comfort, well-being, and morale of the crew.

The new U-boat construction program was assigned top priority as the vehicle for Germany to regain the initiative in the "Battle of the Atlantic." Leading U-boat designers were as-sembled at the small town of Blankenberg in the Harz Mountains, far from interference by Allied air raids. There, a central design agency addressed the problems of bringing the Type XXI into being. Preliminary designs were completed by June, 1943, and the following month the first blueprints were submitted to Dönitz for his approval.

The initial objective was to complete 12 of the new 1600 ton U-boats per month beginning August, 1945. Dönitz objected that such a schedule would provide too few boats too late. He appealed to Germany's Armaments Minister, Albert Speer, who appointed a leading production engineer, Otto Merker, to head the mass pro-duction program. It was a challenging assignment that Merker addressed with a composite program of standardized mass production and pre-fabri-cation. His plan called for pre-assembly of each boat in eight massive sections to be joined together at one of three shipyards. Because the shipyards were prime targets for Allied air strikes, the assembly process was limited to 30 days.

Merker's production build up called for 18

boats to be delivered in July 1944, increasing to 33 per month by October. But his program was plagued by late, incomplete, and inaccurate detail drawings. In addition, destructive air raids were continually shutting down suppliers of diesel engines, battery components, and other materials. By late 1943, Allied reconnaissance had photo-graphed the Type XXI under construction. Intensified air attacks accounted for frequent shipyard work interruptions of three to four weeks. Such bombing of Germany's production network protected Allied navies and seaborne commerce from the formidable new U-boat menace.

An armada of incomplete Type XXI U-boats on the ways of Blohm & Voss shipyard in bomb-shattered Hamburg. The devastated shipyard attests to the effectiveness of the Allied air offensive against the "Super Subs." Courtesy of National Archives.

Pre-fabricated sections of a Type XXI U-boat ready to be assembled. With Germany's surrender in May 1945, this one was never completed. Courtesy of National Archives.

Uniformity and quality standards are difficult to maintain in a decentralized manufacturing program. The production of components for the Type XXI by many unrelated companies proved to be no exception. The final assembly of pre-fabricated hull sections and the installation of engines, cables, pipes, and auxiliary machinery was a lengthy process of trying to fit mis-matched components, then reworking or rejecting them.

Shipyard labor had been heavily hit by demands of the German war effort. Approximately 70% of the skilled workers had been drafted into the military, to be replaced by low-skilled conscript labor. Continued production of the obsolete Type VIIC proved to be a logistical mistake. It diverted essential materials and skills away from production of the new U-boat.

Design changes were no surprise. They were to be expected, particularly on so advanced a concept. But each took its toll of schedule time. In one design decision, surface performance was sacrificed in favor of underwater efficiency. Exhaust-driven diesel superchargers were re-moved rather than to sacrifice the new "schnor-chel" that permitted running just below the surface at twice the six knot speed of earlier U-boats. Arguments flourished regarding twin 30mm anti-aircraft guns at each end of the bridge. The questionable need for surface protection of a boat that was designed for underwater survival was argued. Fortunately, not all controversy resulted in change.

The Type XXI was the first of Germany's U-boats to have six bow torpedo tubes and 23 torpedoes. But an even more important ordnance innovation, a hydraulic torpedo loader, per-mitted reloading all six torpedo tubes in 12 minutes at the press of a button. The earlier Type VIIC required about 15 minutes for a single tube.

Ultrasensitive hydrophones added new listening capabilities within a range of 50 miles. The Balkon Gerät was a highly sophisticated echo chamber that tracked, identified, and ranged multiple targets while the U-boat was submerged. The Type XXI could attack her prey from a depth of 160 feet without having seen or been seen by the

Open and closed bow torpedo tubes of Type XXI U-boats. Note, just beneath the tubes, the large, bulbous Balkon Gerät, the revolutionary underwater sound detection gear. Courtesy of National Archives.

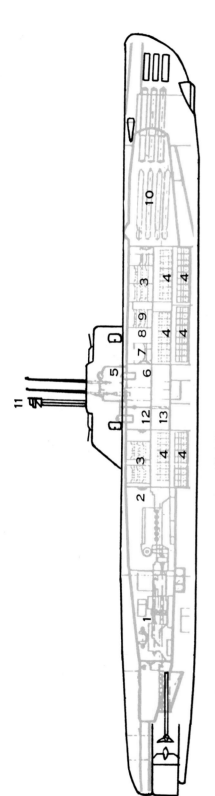

TYPE XXI

1. Electric motor room
2. Diesel engine room
3. Crew quarters
4. Batteries
5. Conning tower
6. Control room
7. Commander's cabin
8. Radio room & listening room
9. Officer's quarters
10. Torpedo room
11. Schnorchel
12. Galley
13. Magazine

Displacement (tons)
  Surfaced 1,621
  Submerged 1,819
Length .... 251'9"
Beam .... 21'9"
Draught .... 20'3"
Fuel capacity (tons) 250
Speed (knots)
  Surfaced 15.6
  Submerged 17.2
Range (nautical miles/kn.)
  Surfaced 15,500/10
  Submerged 285/6
Armament
  Bow torpedo tubes 6
  Stern torpedo tubes 0
  Torpedoes carried (number/size) .... 23/21"
  Guns (number/size) 4/30mm
Crew 57

enemy. The hull was specified to sustain the pressure of 1,000 feet. None of the U-boats attempted that depth but the crew of one boat that was tested to 650 feet, stated that they would have gone to 1,000 feet with full confidence.

Instead of the 18 boats scheduled for July, only one, *U-2501* was completed but she was never made operational. Almost immediately, the first of the new series was returned to the shipyard for repairs. Two others, *U-2511* and *U-3008,* were the only Type XXI's to leave on operational service.

THE WAR ENDS

Adolph Hitler committed suicide on April 30, 1945, the day *U-2511* (Kvtkpt. Schnee) left for operations in the Carribean with orders not to engage enemy vessels during the outbound voyage. En route, the U-boat carried out a mock attack on the heavily guarded British cruiser *Norfolk,* then escaped without detection. The war ended and Schnee was ordered back to base. His was one of only 12 Type XXI boats fully ready for action. In all, there were 121 in the water and over 1,000 were under construction or on order. The contribution of that formidable force would have added a new dimension to the "Battle of the Atlantic," perhaps not to victory but certainly to prolong the struggle.

The war was over and Allied technical missions vied with each other for technical data on the Nazi wonder weapons. Americans and British competed with the Russians who they knew would never share such information. Fortunately for American and British interests, their armies had overrun the port cities of Hamburg, Kiel, and Wilhelmshaven, sites of the most vital technical material on the new U-boat. The Russians had captured Stettin and Danzig. There they found many U-boat hulls in the process of being built but little technical data.

Moving into Bremen on the heels of retreating and surrendering Germans, U.S. forces found sections of the modular construction Type XXI U-boats ready to be assembled. Courtesy of National Archives.

U.S. servicemen inspect a section of a Type XXI U-boat after Germany's capitulation. Courtesy of National Archives.

One of the 121 Type XXI's launched before the war ended was *U-2513*, constructed by Blohm & Voss at Hamburg, Germany in late 1944 — early 1945. It is certain that she made no war cruises and in all probability was never commissioned. With the collapse of Nazi Germany, the new U-boat was surrendered in May, 1945 to the Allies at Horten, Norway, a haven for Baltic Sea U-boats during the last five weeks of the war.

Early in 1946, a Three-Power Agreement provided Britain, France, and the United States each with ten of Germany's U-boats (Appendix H). All others were to be destroyed. One of two Type XXI's assigned to the United States was *U-2513*.

In August 1946, *U-2513* arrived in Charleston, S.C. for extensive overhaul. She left for Key West on September 24th, for six months of design evaluation and duty in conjunction with the development of submarine and anti-submarine tactics. On completion of that assignment the U-boat left Key West for Portsmouth, N.H., to remain there from March 22 till September 8. Six weeks of operation in the U.S. Navy Atlantic Fleet followed. After that duty ended on October 15th, *U-2513* returned to Key West to resume her former role until summer, 1949.

After *U-2513*'s commissioning into the U.S. Navy her new insignia represented both her German past and her present role of protector of America's liberty. One of the U-boat's turret mounted twin 30mm anti-aircraft guns can be seen at the top. Courtesy of National Archives.

Fleet Admiral Chester W. Nimitz inspects *U-2513* on May 11, 1946. Vice Admiral Forrest Sherman has hold of the periscope. Courtesy of U.S. Naval Historical Center.

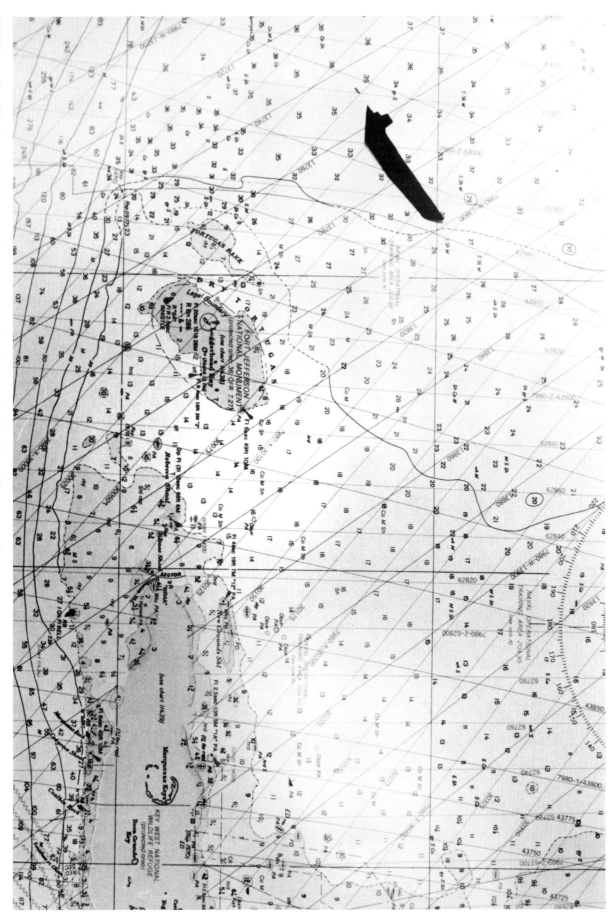

U-2513 was sunk at 24° 53′ N, 83° 15′ W, northeast of the Dry Tortugas. This illustration should not be used for navigational purposes.

THE SINKING

After three years of service *U-2513* had outlived her usefulness to the United States Navy. She was moved to Norfolk, Virginia in mid-June 1949, then to Portsmouth, N.H. to be placed out of service in July. She remained there until August 1951, when it was decided that she would be sunk by naval firing tests. On October 7, 1951, five years after the "Wonder Boat" arrived in the United States, USS *Petrel* (ASR-14), a submarine rescue ship, towed the U-boat to a site off the Dry Tortugas, west of Key West, Florida. The destroyer *Robert A. Owens* (DDK-827) was ordered to sink her as a target for U.S. Navy test rockets. Ironically, her greatest military contribution was, not to the Third Reich, but to the United States by providing her with Germany's advanced, state-of-the-art technical data that was just barely too late to alter the course of World War II.

DIVING HISTORY

Petrel, U-2513's tow to the site of her sinking, returned the following year for sonar, demolition, and diving exercises for 12 Navy divers who made a total of 20 practice dives to the wreck. *Petrel's* log reports the U-boat to be in 228 feet of water. The divers were recorded as having made dives to 194 feet.

U-2513, northeast of the Dry Tortugas at 24°53' N, 83°15' W, awaits her first amateur scuba divers. The depth may seem excessive for sport diving, but dive charters from Key West visit another submarine, the U.S. Navy's *S-16* which lies 240 feet underwater. There is no information that anyone has yet attempted to find *U-2513*. When one does, a first step might be to question local shrimp boat captains about locations at the reported coordinates where nets have snagged. Then, bottom scanning techniques might provide a recognizable profile of the sunken U-boat. Or a search grid pattern might be laid out for methodical screening of the area — at the expense of time and money.

The U-boat lies about 90 miles out of Key West, a lengthy, rather expensive dive charter with no assurance of success for a wreck without exotic cargo, no illustrious war record, and possibly stripped of potential artifacts before she was sunk. But history is represented in what remains of Germany's state-of-the-art World War II U-boat. That is all the appeal needed to whet the appetite of a venturesome diver who aspires to be the first scuba visitor to the relic of another era. Problems, time, and expense serve only to spark the determination of such avid amateur historians. One will, one day, pay his respects to Germany's "Super Sub."

APPENDIX A

NAVAL OFFICER RANK EQUIVALENTS

GERMAN

OFFIZIERE MIT PATENT

Grossadmiral

Generaladmiral

Admiral

Vizeadmiral

Konteradmiral

Kapitän zur See

Kommadore

Fregattenkapitän

Korvettenkapitän

Kapitänleutnant

Oberleutnant zur See

Leutnant zur See

OFFIZIERSNAHWUCHS

Oberfahnrich zur See

Fahnrich zur See

Seekadett

Matrose (Seeoffiziersanwärter)

OFFIZIERE OHNE PATENT

Oberbootsmann

Bootsmann

Oberbootsmaat

Bootsmaat

Obermaschinist

MANNSCHAFTEN

Maschinenmaat

Maschinenobergefreiter

Maschinengefreiter

Oberstabsmatrose, Hauptgefreiter

Stabsmatrose, Matrosenobergefreiter,
   Mechanikerobergefreiter, Funkobergefreiter

Obermatrose, Matrosengefreiter,
   Mechanikergefreiter, Funkgefreiter

Matrose

UNITED STATES

COMMISSIONED OFFICERS

Commander in Chief, Admiral of the Fleet

Admiral, Commander of a Fleet

Admiral

Vice Admiral

Rear Admiral

Captain

Commodore, Courtesy Title (sr. captain)

Commander (junior captain)

Lieutenant Commander

Lieutenant (senior grade)

Lieutenant (junior grade)

Ensign

OFFICER CANDIDATES

Senior Midshipman

Midshipman

Naval Cadet

Seaman (officer's apprentice)

NON-COMMISSIONED OFFICERS

Chief Petty Officer, Chief Boatswain's Mate

Petty Officer, first class, Boatswain's Mate, first
   class

Petty Officer, second class, Boatswain's Mate,
   second class

Petty Officer, third class, Coxswain

Warrant Machinist

ENLISTED PERSONNEL

Fireman, first class

Fireman, second class

Fireman, third class

Able Seaman, first class

Seaman, first class

Seaman, second class

Seaman, Recruit (apprentice)

Obersteuermann	Quartermaster of Warrant rank
Mechaniker	Artificer's Mate, first class, Torpedoman's Mate, first class
Obermechanikersmaat	Artificer's Mate, second class, Torpedoman's Mate, second class
Mechanikersmaat	Artificer's Mate, third class, Torpedoman's Mate, third class
Oberfunkmaat	Radioman, second class
Funkmaat	Radioman, third class

APPENDIX B

LIST OF BODIES RECOVERED FROM U-85

Name	Age	Cemetery Plot*	Rank	U.S.N. Equivalent
Sanger, Hans	31	688	Oberleutnant (Ing.)	Lieutenant (j.g.) engineering duties only
Ungethum Eugen	30	698	Stabsobermaschinist	
Adrian, Heinrich	20	711	Obermaschinist	Warrant machinist
Kaiser, Helmit	26	710	Bootsmaat	Coxswain
Heller, H.	20	689	Maschinenmaat	Fireman 1c1
Kleibrink, Joseph	16-18	692	Maschinengefreiter	Fireman 3c1
Schulze	24	704	"	"
Schultes, Karl	20	700	Matrosengefreiter	Seaman 2c1
Schulz, Günther	22	705	"	"
Albig, Herbert	22	701	Unknown	
Ammann, Gerhard	26	712	"	
Behla	16-18	714	"	
Degenkolb, Erich	25	694	"	
Ganzl	24	697	"	
Hahnefeodt	25	690	"	
Hanson, O.	23	695	"	
Kiefer	23	706	"	
Letzig, Jan	27	699	"	
Metge	21	713	"	
Piotronski, Arthur	22	707	"	
Prantle, O.	21	687	"	
Roeder	25	693	"	
Scheon	23	702	"	
Schumacher, Werner	24	696	"	
Spoddig, Horst	16-18	691	"	
Strobel, Friedrich	26	715	"	
Waack	27	708	"	
Waschman	21	709	"	
Weidmann, Konstantin	25	703	"	

TOTAL: 29

* **Hampton National Cemetery, Hampton, Virginia.**

OFFICERS AND MEN PRESUMED TO BE MEMBERS OF THE CREW OF U-85

Name	Rank	U.S.N Equivalent
Greger, Eberhard	Oberleutnant zur See	Lieutenant (j.g.)
Leghler	"	"
Perret	Obermaschinist	Warrant machinist
Oldoerf	Bootsmaat	Coxswain
Rogge	Maschinenmaat	Fireman 1cl
Guneel	Maschinengefreiter	Fireman3cl
Hagemeier	"	"
Schorch	Matrosengefreiter	Seaman 2cl
Wittmann	Unknown	

APPENDIX C

SURVIVORS OF U-352

Name	Rank	U.S.N Equivalent
Rathke, Hellmut	Kapitänleutnant	Lieutenant
Bernard, Oskar	Leutnant zur See (Sonderführer)	Ensign (acting)
Kammerer, Ernst	Fähnrich zur See	Midshipman
Orandke, Walter	Obermaschinist	Warrant machinist
Bollmann, Heinrich	"	"
Richter, Helmut H.	Bootsmaat	Coxswain
Daern, Arthur	"	"
Neitsch, Hans	"	"
Krekeler, Siegfried	"	"
Wessoly, Lothar	Maschinenmaat	Fireman 1cl
Schwarzenberger, Heins	"	"
Brand, August Michael	"	"
Wesche, Martin William	"	"
Thohnissen, Kurt H.	"	"
Reussel, Gerd*	"	"
Stengel, Otto	Maschinenobergefreiter	Fireman 2cl
Rusch, Gerhard	"	"
Twirdy, Heinrich	Maschinengefreiter	Fireman 3cl
Minzker, Johann	"	"
Richter, Heins Earl	"	"
Sorg, Ludwig	Funkmaat	Radioman 3cl
Krueger, Kurt	"	"
Kominek, Franz	Matrosengefreiter	Seaman 2cl
Pickel, Erhard	"	"
Herrschaft, Edgar	"	"
Henschke, Otto	"	"
Hering, Gerhard	"	"
Heinze, Hans	"	"
Mattiz, Hans	Funkgefreiter	"
Richter, Gerhard	"	"
Thiele, Rudolf	Mechanikergefreiter	"
Link, Wilhelm	Matrose	Apprentice seaman
Staron, Edmund	"	"

TOTAL: 33
* Died due to injuries.

CASUALTIES OF U-352

Name	Rank	U.S.N Equivalent
Tretz, Heinz	Oberleutnant (Ing.)	Lieutenant (j.g.) engineering duties only
Ernst, Jospeh	Leutnant zur See	Ensign
Paineck	Obersteuermann	No equivalent rank
Kuchler	Mechanikermaat	Torpedoman's mate 3cl
Kirschke	Maschinenmaat	Fireman 1cl
Nicholait	Maschinenobergefreiter	Fireman 2cl
Heinrich	Matrosengefreiter	Seaman 2cl
Burutta	"	' "
Scholtze	Mechanikergefreiter	"
Martin	Matrose	Apprentice Seaman
Kupisch	"	"
Sailer	"	"
Kleinholz	"	"

TOTAL: 13

TOTAL CREW OF U-352

Officers	3
Midshipmen	1
Petty Officers	18
Other ranks	24
TOTAL	**46**

APPENDIX D

SURVIVORS OF U-701

Name	Rank	U.S.N Equivalent
Degen, Horst	Kapitänleutnant	Lieutenant
Kunert, Gunter	Obersteuermann	No equivalent rank
Grotheer, Herbert	Funkmaat	Radioman 3cl
Vaüpel, Ludwig	Maschinenmaat	Fireman 1cl
Seldte, Werner	Mechanikergefreiter	Seaman 2cl
Schwendel, Gerhardt	"	"
Faust, Bruno	"	"
TOTAL: 7		

CASUALTIES OF U-701

Name	Rank	U.S.N Equivalent
Junker, Konrad	Oberleutnant zur See	Lieutenant (j.g.)
Bahr, Karl-Heinrich	Oberleutnant (Ing.)	Lieutenant (j.g.), engineering duties only
Basies	Leutnant zur See	Ensign
*Lange	Fähnrich (Ing.)	Ensign, engineering duties only
Fritz, Walter	Obermaschinist	Warrant machinist
Köwing, Kurt	"	"
Gründler	Oberbootsmaat	Boatswain's mate 2cl
Hänsel, Kurt (?)	"	"
Birnmeyer	Bootsmaat	Coxswain
Etzweiler	"	"
Höhlein	Funkmaat	Radioman 3cl
Weber	Machanikermaat	Torpedoman's mate 3cl
Damrow	Maschinenmaat	Fireman 1cl
*Bosse	"	"
Fischer	"	"
Schuller	"	"
*Gross	Matrosenobergefreiter	Seaman 1cl
Weiland	"	"

Peters	Matrosengefreiter	Seaman 2cl
Löwe, Paul	,,	,,
Magg, Xavier	,,	,,
Amrhein	,,	,,
Stadler	,,	,,
Wallaschek	,,	,,
Raddatz	,,	,,
Kundt	,,	,,
Dominik	Funkgefreiter	,,
Ermitario	,,	,,
Schmidtmeyer	Maschinengefreiter	Fireman 3cl
Brannig	,,	,,
*Lauffeidt	,,	,,
Hoppe	,,	,,
Laskowski	Matrose	Apprentice seaman
*Leu	,,	,,
Miehalek	,,	,,
*Nimsch	,,	,,

TOTAL: 36
* Joined U-701 for the last cruise.

TOTAL CREW OF U-701

Officers	4
Midshipmen	1
Petty Officers	15
Other ranks	23
TOTAL	**43**

APPENDIX E

CASUALTIES OF U-853

Name	Age	Rank	U.S.N. Equivalent
Frömsdorf, Helmut	24	Oberleutnant zur See	Lieutenant (j.g.)
Poorten, Gotthart	23	Oberleutnant zur See	,,
Abele, Hans Ulrich	22	Leutnant zur See	Ensign
Schencke, Wolfgang	22	,,	,,
Wilde, Christian	26	Leutnant (Ing.)	Ensign, engineering duties only
Kistner, Heinrich	24	Obersteuermann	No equivalent rank
Fehrs, Helmut	29	Obermaschinist	Warrant machinist
Wolf, Nikolaus	26	,,	,,
Greiner, Rudolf	23	Obermaschinistmaat	?
Merker, Willi	22	,,	?
Wüst, Karl	23	,,	?
Lyhs, Johann	23	Bootsmaat	Coxswain
Schwenk, Theo	24	,,	,,
Hölzer, Herbert	21	Maschinenmaat	Fireman 1cl
Liescher, Willibald	24	,,	,,
Meier, Helmut	22	,,	,,
Winkler, Herbert	23	,,	,,
Brdlik, Siegfried	20	Maschinenobergereiter	Fireman 2cl
Bühler, Hermann	20	,,	,,
Corbach, Anton	19	,,	,,
Edler, Herbert	20	,,	,,
Geissler, Heinz	25	,,	,,
Hazalik, Erich	21	,,	,,
Klein, Josef	20	,,	,,
Luckei, Gunter	19	,,	,,
Nasse, Franz	20	,,	,,
Reister, Berthold	20	,,	,,
Rosemann, Heinrich	22	,,	,,
Schwarz, Helmut	20	,,	,,
Volk, Friedrich	21	,,	,,
Wulle, Willibald	20	,,	
Pokel, Walter	?	Maschinengefreiter	Fireman 3cl

Bartsch, Eugen	19	Matrosenobergefreiter	Seaman 1cl
Bereskin, Arthur	22	"	"
Dörwald, Paul	20	"	"
Gari, Oskar	24	"	"
Hoffman, Herbert	22	"	"
Lehmann, Rudolf	23	"	"
Mruck, Helmut	21	"	"
Suchy, Herbert	22	"	"
Porstner, Franz	20	Mechanikerobergefreiter	"
Schumann, Werner	20	"	"
Herbert, Rudolf	19	Funkobergefreiter	"
Schanz, Lothar	20	"	"
Böhme, Egon	19	Mechanikergefreiter	Seaman 2cl
Mieschliwietz, Helmut	18	Matrosengefreiter	Seaman 2cl
Rosenmüller, Helmut	19	"	"
Trotz, Alfred	19	"	"
Zacher, Karl-Heinz	18	"	"
Rauch, Egon	19	Funkgefreiter	"
Warster, Karl	21	Funkmaat	Radioman 3cl
Heiligtag, Kurt	25	Mechanikermaat	Torpedoman's Mate 3cl
Grahl, Werner	22	San. Mt.	?
Schaadt, Erich	29	Ob. Fk. Mstr.	?
Schmidt, Kurt	22	Str. Mt.	?

APPENDIX F

Visual distance calculations at sea are approximated by a navigational formula that makes provision for the curvature of the earth. To estimate the distance in nautical miles (6,080 feet) from a point of observation to the horizon (disappearance point), multiply the square root of the altitude (feet above sea level) by 1.144:

1. Assuming that the observation point is 18 feet above sea level, determine the square root of 18 (4.24).
2. Multiply by 1.144 to establish the distance to the horizon (4.85 nautical miles).

If an observed object is beyond the horizon, an additional calculation is needed to determine its distance from the point of observation. The height of the lowest observed point of the object is required, to serve as a hypothetical point of observation looking back at the horizon, using the same navigational formula as above. The result, added to the original calculation, provides the approximate total distance in nautical miles from the point of observation to the lowest observed point of the object:

1. If a point 280 feet high is visible just above the horizon from an observation point 18 feet above sea level, calculate the distance from the observer to the horizon (4.85).
2. Calculate the square root of 280 (16.73).
3. Multiply by 1.144 = 19.14 nautical miles beyond the horizon to the observed object.
4. Add the distance to the horizon (4.85) and the distance beyond the horizon (19.14) = 23.99 (24) nautical miles from an observation point 18 feet above sea level to a point 280 high, seen just above the horizon.

APPENDIX G

DISPOSITION OF U-BOATS IN
U.S. CUSTODY AFTER WORLD WAR I.

U-Boat	Type	Where	When	How
U-111	Ms	In 266 fathoms	1922	?
U-117	UEII	50 miles east of Cape Charles Vir. (beyond 50 fathom line)	7/22/21	Aerial bombardment
U-140	U-cruiser	Same location as *U-117*	7/22/21	Aerial bombardment and gunfire from USS *Dickerson (DD-157)*
UB-88	UBIII	Off California	3/1/21	Gunfire from USS *Wickes (DD-75)*
UB-148	UBIII	Same location as *U-117* & *U-140*	7/22/21	Aerial bombardment and gunfire from USS *Sicard (DD-346)*
UC-97	UCIII	Lake Michigan (42°10' N, 87°20' W)	6/7/21	Gunfire from USS *Willmette*

APPENDIX H

DISPOSITION OF U-BOATS IN
U.S. CUSTODY AFTER WORLD WAR II.

U-Boat	Type	Where	When	How
U-234	XB	40 miles NE of Cape Cod, Mass., in 600' of water	11/20/47	By USS *Greenfish* (SS-542) in torpedo exploder test
U-505	IXC	Museum of Science & Industry, Chicago	9/25/55	By private subscription
U-530	IXC$_{40}$	40 miles NE of Cape Cod, Mass., in 600' of water	11/20/47	By USS *Toro* (SS-422) in torpedo exploder test
U-858	IXC$_{40}$	40 miles NE of Cape Cod, Mass., in 600' of water	11/20/47	By Submarine Force in torpedo exploder test
U-873	IXD$_2$	New York City	3/10/48	Sold for scrap to private industry
U-889	IXC$_{40}$	40 miles NE of Cape Cod, Mass., in 600' of water	11/20/47	By Submarine Force in torpedo exploder test
U-977	VIIC	Off Cape Cod, Mass.	11/13/46	By USS *Atule* (SS-403) in torpedo exploder test
U-1105	VIIC	Off Virginia 38N, 67W	9/19/49	Sunk during demolition tests
U-1406	XVIIB	New York City	5/18/48	Sold for scrap to private industry
U-2513	XXI	Off Dry Tortugas 24°53'N, 83°15' W	10/7/51	Sunk during rocket firing tests
U3008	XXI	Portsmouth, N.H.	9/15/55	Sold for scrap to Loudes Iron & Metal Co.
U-805	IXC$_{40}$	Off Massachusetts, 42°32'N, 69°37'W	2/5/46	Sunk in over 100 fathoms
U-1228	IXC$_{40}$	Off Massachusetts, 42°32'N, 69°37'W	2/5/46	Sunk in over 100 fathoms

All operational types of U-boats are represented in the preceding list except Type XXIII, a prefabricated type boat of 234 tons, and Type XIV, a 1,600-ton supply boat called "U-Tanker." This boat is not to be confused with the 1,600-ton mine layer and supply submarine *U-234*. The Type XIV was particularly vulnerable to attack and it is believed that all of them were lost in war operations.

The United States was originally allocated two type XXIII U-boats which were among five submarines allocated States but located in Europe. The United States requested that U-boats already in the Western Hemisphere be substituted for those in Europe. The only exception was *U-1105,* an experimental boat with a rubber hull covering, which the United States Navy wanted for experimental purposes. Her hull was covered with rubber to deaden sonar pulses and was known as the "Black Panther."

U-1406 is one of the two Type XVIIB (Walter boats) which were salvaged at Kiel after having been scuttled by the Germans.

The United States was the only one of the Allies to receive a Type IXD 2, U-boat *(U-873)*. These boats had a long cruising range and were intended originally for operation in the Indian Ocean and South African waters. Later they were converted into submarine blockade runners.

U-505 was captured by USN forces on June 4, 1944, about 150 miles off the coast of Rio De Oro, Africa. After the war's end Congress authorized the U-boat be given to the Museum of Science and Industry in Chicago.

According to an agreement reached by the Allies that all unallocated U-boats were to be sunk, *U-1228* and *U-805*, the only unallocated U-boats in American waters, with the exception of *U-505*, were sunk in February 1946.

BIBLIOGRAPHY

Allen, Tom. "Mystery At 20 Fathoms." New York *Sunday News,* January 22, 1961, February 5, 1961.

Archer, William. *The Pirate's Progress: A Short History of the U-boat.* Harper & Brothers Publishers, 1918.

Bagnasco, Erminio. *Submarines of World War Two.* U.S. Naval Institute Press, 1977.

Barck, Jr., Oscar, and Blake, Nelson. *Since 1900.* The Macmillan Co., 1959.

Bekker, Cajus. *Hitler's Naval War.* Doubleday & Co., Inc., 1974.

Blair, Jr., Clay. *Silent Victory.* J.B. Lippincott Co., 1975.

"The Bones in U-853." *Newsweek,* July 4, 1960.

Botting, Douglas. *The U-Boats.* Time Life Books, 1979.

Brodie, Bernard and Fawn. *From Crossbow to H-Bomb.* Dell Publishing Co., Inc., 1962.

Buchheim, Gunther. *The Boat.* Bantam Books, 1976.

Bunch, Jim. "A Dive Into WWII History Off North Carolina Coast." *Skin Diver,* April 1980.

Burgess, Robert F. *Ships Beneath The Sea: A History of Subs and Submersibles.* McGraw-Hill Book Co., 1975.

Busch, Harold. *U-boats At War.* Putnam, 1955.

Churchill, Winston. *The Second World War.* Houghton Mifflin, 1948-53.

Clark, William Bell. *When U-boats Came to America.* Little Brown & Co., 1929.

Creswell, John. *Sea Warfare.* Univ. of California Press, 1967.

Degen, Horst. "The Last Voyage of the U-701." *Eagle,* August, 1982.

— "Open Sea Hunt." *Eagle,* October 1982.

— "Attack and Escape." *Eagle,* December 1982.

— "Final Accounting." *Eagle,* February 1983.

DeWan, George. "WWII The Last Good War." *Newsday,* May 5, 1985.

Dickerson, Michael T. "Saga of the U-352: The Unluckiest Sub." *Skin Diver,* November 1981.

Dictionary of American Naval Fighting Ships. Naval History Division, Office of the Chief of Naval Operations, 1969.

Dönitz, Admiral Karl. *Memoirs: Ten Years and Twenty Days.* Leisure Books, 1959.

Dupuy, R. Ernest and Trevor N. *The Encyclopedia of Military History.* Harper and Row, 1977.

Fitzsimons, Bernard. *The Illustrated Encyclopedia of 20th Century Weapons and Warfare.* Columbia House.

Frank, Wolfgang. *The Sea Wolves.* Ballantine Books, 1972.

Fulton, Garland. "A Chapter In The History of Submarines." *U.S. Naval Institute Proceedings,* January 1941.

Gasaway, E.B. *Grey Wolf, Grey Sea.* Ballatine Books, Inc., 1970.

Gibson, R.H. and Prendergast, Maurice. *The German Submarine War.* Richard R. Smith, Inc., 1931.

Goodwin, Derek V. and Freicherr, Greg. "Torpedoes Off Shore: U-Boats That Won't Die." *Rocky Mountain News-Parade The Sunday Newspaper Magazine,* April 22, 1979.

Gray, Edwyn A. *The Killing Time: The German U-boats 1914-1918.* Scribner's Sons, 1972.

Hausrath, Ralph. "The U-853 Is Still On Patrol." *Long Island Forum,* May 1980.

Hoehling, A.A. *The Great War at Sea.* Galahad Books, 1965.

Hoyt, Edwin P. *U-Boats Offshore.* Stein & Day, 1978.

Hughes, Terry and Costello, John. *The Battle of the Atlantic.* Dial Press, 1977.

Kearney, Thomas A. "The Submarine: Its Purpose and Development." *U.S. Naval Institute Proceedings,* 1915.

Keith, Donald H., Greneker, Gene, and Lovin, Bill. "Time Bomb On The Bottom." *Skin Diver,* June 1976.

Kurzak, Karl Heinz. "German U-Boat Construction." *U.S. Naval Institute Proceedings,* April 1955.

Lyon, D.J. and H.J. *World War II Warships.* Excalibur Books.

Lenton, H.T. *Navies of the Second World War: German Submarines 1.* Doubleday & Company, Inc., 1967.

— *Navies of the Second World War: German Submarines 2.* Doubleday & Company, Inc., 1967.

Manchester, William. *The Arms of Krupp 1587-1968.* Little Brown & Co., 1968.

Marshall, S.L.A. *World War I.* American Heritage Press, 1964.

Mason, David. *U-Boat: The Secret Menace.* Ballantine Books Inc., 1968

McCombs, D. and Worth, Fred L. *World War II Super Facts.* Warner Books, 1983.

Moffat, Alexander W. *A Navy Maverick Comes of Age, 1939-1945.* Walyan, 1977.

Morison, Samuel Eliot. *History of U.S. Naval Operations in WWII, Vol. X, The Atlantic Battle Won, May 1943 — May 1945.* Little Brown & Co., 1956.

Noli, Jean. *The Admiral's Wolf Pack.* Doubleday & Company, Inc., 1974.

Offley, Ed. "Two Old Soldiers Redeem Bonds of War." *Greensboro News and Record,* July 11, 1982.

ONI 250 Series, a series of postmortem studies on enemy submarines sunk in U.S. waters. Naval History Division. Office of the Chief of Naval Operations.

Preston, Antony. *U-Boats.* Excalibur Books, 1978.

— *Submarines.* Bison Books, Inc., 1982.

Roach, Thomas and Subervi, Elliot. "The Twisted Fate of the *U-853.*" *Skin Diver,* March 1974.

Rohwer, J. and Hummelchen, G. *Chronology of the War at Sea 1939-1945.* Arco Publishing Co., Inc., 1974.

Rossler, Eberhard. *The U-boat: The Evolution and Technical History of German Submarines.* Arms and Armour Press, 1981.

Rouse, Jr., Parke. "Under the Cloak of Night." *U.S. Naval Institute Proceedings,* June 1982.

Shirer, William L. *20th Century Journey, Vol. II: The Nightmare Years, 1930-1940.* Little Brown and Co., 1984.

Segal, Jonathan. "Diving Into Coffin of German U-boat." *Gastonia Gazette,* July 29, 1979.

Showell, J.P.M. *U-Boats Under the Swastika.* Arco Publishing Co., Inc., 1977.

Stark, Timothy B. "Hoist Surveys U-352." *Faceplate.*

Stern, Robert C. *U-Boats In Action.* Squadron/Signal Publications, Inc., 1977.

The Story of the U-505. Museum of Science & Industry, Chicago, 1955.

Thomas, Lowell. *Raiders of the Deep.* Doubleday, Doran and Company, 1928.

Tollaksen, D.M. "Last Chapter for U-853." *U.S. Naval Institute Proceedings,* December 1960.

U.S. Naval Technical Mission In Europe, Technical Report No. 312-45, German Submarine Design, 1939-1945. Unpublished report in Operational Archives Branch, Naval Historical Center, Washington Navy Yard.

Werner, Herbert A. *Iron Coffins.* Holt, Rinehart and Winston, 1969.

Winterbotham, F.W. *The Ultra Secret.* Dell Publishing Co., Inc., 1975.

INDEX

183